A PHOTOGRAPHIC GUIDE TO

Wildflowers of Outback Australia

DENISE GREIG

Published in Australia in 2002 by
New Holland Publishers (Australia) Pty Ltd
Sydney • Auckland • London • Cape Town

Unit 1/66 Gibbes St Chatswood NSW 2067 Australia
218 Lake Road Northcote Auckland New Zealand
86 Edgware Road London W2 2EA United Kingdom
Wembly Square First Floor Solan Street Gardens Cape Town 8000 South Africa

National Library of Australia Cataloguing-in-Publication Data:

Greig, Denise, 1945-2010.
        A photographic guide to wildflowers of Outback Australia.
        Includes index.
        ISBN 9781864368055

        1. Wild flowers — Australia — Pictorial works.
        2. Wild flowers — Australia — Identification. I. Title.
        (Series: Photoguides)

        582.130994

Publisher: Louise Egerton
Project Editor: Yani Silvana
Editor: Anne Savage
Designer: Alix Korte
Cover Design: Alix Korte
Cartographer: Ian Faulkner
Production Controller: Wendy Hunt
Reproduction: Sang Choy International, Singapore
Printer: Toppan Leefung Printing Ltd, China

Picture credits
(t = top, b = bottom)
Tim Low: p. 40, p. 44b, p. 114, p. 123t & b,
        p. 124, p. 126b, p. 131 t & b, p. 133t
Murray Fagg: p. 34
NHIL/Jaime Plaza van Roon: p. 108b, p. 109t

CONTENTS

INTRODUCTION

The term 'outback' means different things to different people — but it usually refers to that part of Australia where you need to be deadly serious about carrying water and wearing sun protection. It is also called the bush, the never-never, the mulga, the back of Bourke and the back of beyond. It is where properties are called stations and where you will see spectacular gorges, ancient river courses, magnificent ghost gums, scenic canyons, treeless plains, continuous carpets of everlastings and many kilometres of country covered with spinifex.

A major advantage of studying wildflowers in outback Australia is that you seldom have to travel far in order to enjoy them. Many visitors expect to see red stony plains swept bare by the wind and devoid of plant life. This may be true if you travel in mid-summer after a prolonged dry spell. However, most people choose to journey through Australia's heart during the cooler months, when it is possible to travel on many inland roads in a conventional car. This is the most pleasant time to travel inland, and after good autumn or winter rain the starkness of the outback can be softened and transformed into a beautiful wildflower garden.

This photographic guide covers around 240 common species of wildflowers you are most likely to encounter growing wild in the accessible or regularly visited parts of outback Australia. Some species are widespread and common in all States, while others may be an important component of a small geographical area. There are some species also found in coastal or forested areas.

Each wildflower selected is individually treated with a colour photograph, descriptive information, habitat notes and a line drawing. Aboriginal plant usage is also recorded where applicable.

Australia's native flora consists of about 18 000 species of flowering plants, grouped in about 200 families of widely varying size. Within the confines of this small book we cannot include all the species you might find growing in the outback, but at least you might discover to which genus the flower belongs and this information will assist you in further study of the plant. This guide is not designed to sit in the bookcase. It is small enough to take up permanent residence in your camera bag, picnic basket or backpack, or in the glovebox of the car, so that you have it for handy reference.

Being able to identify and call a plant by its name helps us to appreciate and gain knowledge of the beautiful and interesting flora of the Australian outback. Hopefully visitors to this country will also find this book a helpful introduction to our magnificent plant life.

In the interests of conservation, do not pick the flowers. It is illegal to pick or dig up any plants in a national park or nature reserve.

THE AREA COVERED BY THIS GUIDE

The term 'outback' refers to remote, thinly inhabited areas of inland Australia. It is generally applied to the semi-arid and arid inland portion of eastern Australia west of the Great Dividing Range. In Western Australia the outback includes the arid centre known as the Eremean Province, and takes in the colourful and accessible mulga country of the Murchison region and the semi-arid intermediate zone known as the Western Australian goldfields or Coolgardie Botanical District. The greater region of Central Australia, which contains Uluru (Ayers Rock) and the Macdonnell, Musgrave and Petermann Ranges and four major deserts, the Gibson, the Great Sandy, the Great Victoria and the Tanami, is often called the 'red centre'. The Nullarbor Plain, the Lake Eyre District and the Flinders Ranges form part of the southern outback.

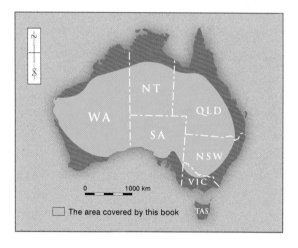

The area covered by this book

HOW TO USE THIS GUIDE

For easy reference, small illustrations showing characteristics common to each family or different groups within a family are featured in the Key to Symbols on page 11. These same illustrations appear in the top corner of pages with species descriptions; similar species are grouped together.

Plant families, and within them, genera and then species, are arranged in alphabetical order, according to their botanical names. *Acacia* (Mimosaceae) is the exception, being arranged in three groups according to flower shape and leaf/phyllode structure. Poaceae, the family to which the grasses belong, is in a section on its own at the end.

Headings

Common names are listed where they are known. Where scientific names have recently changed, former ones (synonyms) are also given.

The Wildflowers Described

The species described and illustrated are those you are most likely to see in often-frequented places in outback Australia. The text deals only with flowering plants, concentrating on grasses, annuals, herbaceous plants and shrubs. Only a few trees are listed. The main description of each plant emphasises prominent characteristics that might be useful in the identification of the species in question, namely height, stems, leaves, inflorescences and flowers, and fruits. Brief reference is made to habitat and geographical distribution, which may help to confirm the identification. Flowering often varies from year to year and bushfires and rainfall patterns can often influence the flowering period.

The Photographs

All species entries are illustrated with a photograph. In most cases the plant is shown in flower, since this is the stage at which it is most obvious and when you are most likely to want to identify it. Every attempt has been made to select photographs which show diagnostic features or which convey the overall character of the plant. Although most of the plants were photographed in their natural habitats, in some cases cultivated plants have had to be used.

Photographs are often the easiest tool for identifying a species. When you have found a photograph in the book that appears to represent the plant, it is a good idea to check whether any of the other photos provide a better match. Finally, read the text, which provides an abbreviated description of the features deemed necessary for correct identification. A good quality hand-lens for observing the fine details of the plant will occasionally be useful.

Line Drawings

Most of the plants described in this book are illustrated by a line drawing of a mature leaf. Leaf shape can be extremely variable, however, and the drawings are no more than a rough guide. For the eucalypts, line drawings of the capsules are provided instead of adult leaves, which in many species do not differ greatly. The shape and size of the capsule and the outline of the valves often help to identify eucalypts. Saltbushes and bluebushes (Chenopodiaceae) have distinctive and typical fruiting bodies which are illustrated in preference to the leaves.

Terminology

Where possible, obscure botanical terminology has been avoided, but commonly used terms such as 'sessile' (without a stalk) and 'terminal' (at the end of the branches) are used throughout. To avoid repeating unnecessary phrases and to keep the text concise, but comprehensible, I have used a mixture of everyday and technical language. A glossary is provided at the back of the book to help you to understand some of these terms. In some cases the meaning of a certain term may be clarified by referring to the line drawing of a particular plant.

THE MAJOR VEGETATION
TYPES OF OUTBACK AUSTRALIA

Each species description mentions a wildflower's preferred vegetation type. Understanding these zones will help you to discover which plants you can expect to find in a specific zone. Most parts of the Australian interior are well vegetated; even the most arid parts have a plant cover of some kind. Ecologists have devised complex and detailed classifications for plant communities and the outlines presented here are simply a general guide.

Woodland

There are three main types of woodland in Australia: tropical woodland, which extends across northern Australia; temperate eucalypt woodland in the south-west and south-east and semi-arid and arid woodland further inland.

Woodland has a more open formation than the denser wet and dry sclerophyll forests of coastal regions. The trees are numerous but their trunks are shorter and the canopy cover is less than 30 per cent. The dominant trees are chiefly eucalypts, and occasionally species of *Casuarina*, *Callitris*, *Melaleuca* and *Acacia*.

The understorey in woodland varies according to region, rainfall, soil nutrients and available sunlight. In drier areas the understorey is often dominated by saltbushes and bluebushes; species of *Acacia* and *Eremophila* provide interest and colour.

Open woodland, where grasses are continuous and well developed, is known as savannah woodland. The trees may be continuous or in small stands and the grasses might include species of *Themeda*, *Stipa*, *Aristida* and other genera. Competing with this grassy layer is a variety of annual and perennial herbs, vines and subshrubs.

Mallee Shrubland

This covers vast semi-arid areas of southern Australia, extending from western Victoria and south-western New South Wales across South Australia to Western Australia. Single-trunked trees are replaced by several species of shrubby eucalypts with multiple stems arising from an underground rootstock known as a lignotuber. The word 'mallee' is an Aboriginal term for a eucalypt from whose roots drinking water could be obtained. The Western Australian goldfields area, where the annual rainfall is about 250 mm, is particularly rich in shrubby eucalypt species. Many of these have large colourful flowers, making them valuable ornamental plants in dry inland towns as well as in arid lands overseas.

The understorey is most commonly dominated by one or more species of *Eremophila*. This genus has a wealth of colourful spring flowers. In fact the genus name is derived from the Greek words *eremos* (a desert) and *philo* (to love), referring to the semi-arid and arid habitats of many of the species. They are able to withstand severe drought and often display leaf adaptations such as a coating of a varnish-like substance, or fine hairs, to ward off the effect of drying winds.

Acacia Shrubland

This type of shrubland comprises a plant community widespread over much of inland Australia, in which small trees or shrubs of the genus *Acacia* are dominant rather than *Eucalyptus*. The plants range from 2 to 10 m in height and by far the most common is the Mulga, *Acacia aneura*, but other wattles of similar habit may be associated with it and are collectively called mulgas. Their leaves have become modified into flattened or needle-like phyllodes to help reduce water loss, a feature that enables acacias to survive better in drier regions than eucalypts.

The name 'mulga' is derived from an Aboriginal word for a long narrow shield made from the wood of *A. aneura*. The word is also used to describe the acacia shrubland populated with these wattles. 'The mulga' is also an Aussie English term applied to any remote inland district, whether it has mulga in it or not.

Low Shrubland

Low shrubland is dominated by saltbush and bluebush shrubs up to 2 m tall intermixed with a few scattered trees and low shrubs such as wattles. This type of vegetation is characteristic of the shrubland found on the Nullarbor Plain, with the most conspicuous plant being the silvery-leaved Pearl Bluebush, *Maireana sedifolia*. In times of drought it might stand alone with bare pinkish-brown earth between, but in a good season it may form part of a rich ground cover of short-lived annuals, grasses, everlastings, pea flowers and numerous herbs.

Grasslands

Grasslands occur mostly in arid and semi-arid zones. Trees may be sparse or absent. Tussock grassland, which covers vast areas of northern Australia from the Kimberley to the Barkly Tableland, is characterised by clumps of several different kinds of *Astrebla*, or Mitchell grasses. Another distinctive grassland formation in the central arid part of Australia is hummock grassland, dominated by large perennial tussocks of species of the incredibly prickly grasses *Trioda* and *Plectrachne*, which form low scattered clumps, and are commonly referred to as spinifex or porcupine grass.

If left unburnt many types of spinifex continually grow outwards throughout their lives. As one of the outer branches bends downwards, it takes root and forms a new plant. This is why you may see large mature clumps forming rings or crescent shapes with the older growth dying off in the centre or on one side.

PLANT IDENTIFICATION MADE EASIER

Wildflowers show considerable variation in the structure of the different parts — leaves, flowers and fruits — when the whole range of Australian species is taken into consideration. Even individuals of the same species that are growing close to each other may show considerable variation in leaf size, shape and hairiness, as well as in the number of branchlets, leaves, flowers and fruits. At the same time, closely related species may be very similar, differing only in small details; accurate identification then becomes quite a challenge. It is usually necessary to identify plants through a combination of features.

Habit

This refers to the form of a plant, whether herb, shrub or tree, and its general appearance, including shape, size, type of growth and the arrangement of various parts. The height is the range of the upper limit that the plant normally attains. Growth rate and final size vary considerably with age and environmental factors such as soil type and the degree of exposure. For prostrate species that always grow along the ground, length may be given instead of height.

Leaves

A leaf is usually green and typically consists of a leaf stalk (petiole) and a flattened leaf blade (lamina). It is the principal food-manufacturing organ of a green plant. Leaves are sometimes distinctive enough to permit identification and subsequent recognition of the species. As well as leaf size, shape and their arrangement on the stem, there are several finer distinguishing features such as colour variation of upper and lower surface, prominence of veins, the presence of oil glands, hairs, scales, stipules, prickles or thorns that you can check. Use of a hand-lens is helpful when checking small structures. In this book leaf measurements refer to the average mature size of the blade (not including the stalk). Remember that almost all plants have both large and some very small leaves.

Flowers and Their Function

The flowers of each species are adapted in shape, structure, colour, the availability of pollen and nectar, and sometimes odour, to help attract their particular pollinating agents, which may be birds, mammals or insects, as well as wind and water. The overall shape of the flower is largely determined by the petals, which are collectively known as the corolla. Within the petals are the stamens; these are male reproductive organs and consist of a sac-like anther that contains the pollen and is supported on a slender stalk. In the centre of the flower is the female reproductive organ, comprising the stigma, style and ovary; together they are called the carpel or pistil. The stigma acts as the receptive surface for pollen grains. The ovary contains varying numbers of ovules, which after fertilisation develop into seeds. The ovary wall develops into the fruit.

The flower provides the most constant and convenient features for identification. These include the sepals and petals, the number of stamens, the type of pistil, the position of the ovary, the number of carpels and ovules, the type of fruit and the symmetry of the flower. Petals and sepals may be present or absent or joined in many ways. In many Australian wildflowers, the flowers themselves are small, but are aggregated into a large showy head (inflorescence). In this guide the arrangement of the inflorescence and dimensions are given where applicable.

Fruit

The term 'fruit' refers to all seed-dispersing structures and is briefly described within the species identifications. Appearance and structure of fruits vary, ranging from small single-seeded nutlets to many-seeded berries and large woody capsules. Fruits can be classified in a number of ways. A simple, practical classification is to divide the fruits into two categories — dry fruits, such as pods and nuts, and fleshy succulent fruits, such as drupes and berries. If the fruit opens at maturity it is called dehiscent, otherwise it is indehiscent.

Key to Symbols

Pigface Family
p. 12

Saltbush Family
p. 41

Wattles Group 2
p. 66

Hop Bush Family
p. 120

Amaranth Family
p. 13

Family Chloanthaceae
p. 46

Wattles Group 3
p. 76

Speedwell Family
p. 122

Amaryllis Family
p. 17

Guinea Flower Family
p. 47

Boobialla Family
p. 78

Potato Family
p. 123

Daisy Family
p. 18

Pea Family
p. 48

Myrtle Family
p. 92

Kurrajong Family
p. 128

Forget-me-not Family
p. 33

Goodenia Family
p. 54

Pittosporum Family
p. 105

Violet Family
p. 129

Brunonia Family
p. 34

Mint Family
p. 59

Parakeelya Family
p. 106

Grass Family
p. 130

Senna Family
p. 35

Mistletoe Family
p. 60

Protea Family
p. 107

Bluebell Family
p. 39

Hibiscus Family
p. 61

Buttercup Family
p. 117

Caper Family
p. 40

Wattles Group 1
p. 64

Citrus Family
p. 118

Pigface Family
AIZOACEAE

Inland Pigface *Carpobrotus modestus*

This is the only inland species of *Carpobrotus*. It is fairly common in mallee scrub. It is a prostrate perennial herb with rooting stems forming a mat to 3 m across. The strongly 3-angled fleshy **leaves** to 7 cm long are dark green or glaucous with reddish tinges and taper to a point. The light purple **flowers** to 2 cm across shade to white at the centre. They appear mostly in spring and s u m m e r, followed by oblong berry-like **fruit** to 2 cm long that is purple when ripe. The fruit and leaves of some *Carpobrotus* species were eaten by Aborigines and explorers. Vic. SA, WA.

Round-leaved Pigface *Disphyma crassifolium*

This species is widespread in salt marshes and sand dunes in coastal areas, and also inhabits inland salt pans where it may form extensive mats. It is a fleshy prostrate perennial herb with trailing stems to 1.5 m long taking root at the leaf nodes. The usually clustered, fleshy green **leaves** 2–5 cm long are club-shaped and almost cylindrical, often tinged yellow or reddish towards the tip. The light purple **flowers** are paler towards the centre and to 3 cm across when opened. They are borne on short stalks in spring and summer. Qld, NSW, Vic, Tas, SA, WA.

AMARANTHACEAE

Crimson Foxtail *Ptilotus atriplicifolius*

Widespread and relatively common in inland woodland communities on sandy or stony ground, this perennial subshrub to 1 m high has stems covered with short dense white hairs. It has obovate grey-green, somewhat wavy **leaves**, 1–5 cm long and to 4 cm wide, with a dense covering of star-shaped hairs. The reddish-purple **flowers** are covered with grey and white hairs and borne in rounded or cylindrical flowerheads to 3 cm diameter and about 5 cm long. These appear at the ends of the stems throughout most of the year. All mainland States.

Weeping Mulla Mulla *Ptilotus calostachyus*

This wispy short-lived perennial herb grows to 2 m high. It occurs in open plains and woodland in the northern part of the red centre. It has smooth stems and sparse linear or thread-like **leaves** 2–6 cm long. The profuse cone-shaped spikes of **flowers** with pointed tips, to 2–8 cm long and about 1.5 cm in diameter, are borne at the ends of pendulous wiry stems in winter and spring. Individual flowers are pink with a dense covering of woolly hairs. Qld, WA, NT.

13

Tall Mulla Mulla *Ptilotus exaltatus*

After good rains this widespread perennial herb to 1.5 m high often forms large showy drifts in open scrub and mulga country. It has rather thick, obovate or lanceolate **leaves** 2–8 cm long ending with a fine point. They are hairy when young and become smaller on the upper stems. The flower-heads are at first cone-shaped but lengthen to become elongated and cylindrical, 3–20 cm long and to 4.5 cm in diameter. The individual **flowers** are deep pink and densely clothed with silky hairs, except on the tips. Flowering time is throughout spring to early summer. All mainland States.

Green Pussytails *Ptilotus macrocephalus*

This erect perennial herb is usually unbranched. It grows to 50 cm high and is widespread in a variety of habitats and on various soils, from red sandy soils to clay, and on low rocky hillsides. It has linear to narrow–lanceolate **leaves** to 5 cm long with wavy margins and a pointed tip. The lightly fragrant, oblong to cylindrical terminal **flower spikes** are up to 12 cm long and 6 cm in diameter, and are borne from spring through to early autumn. Individual flowers are yellowish-green and covered with long hairs. All mainland States.

14

Yellowtails *Ptilotus nobilis*

Widely distributed in drier regions and found in a wide range of habitats, this stout perennial herb to 1 m high shoots from a deep root system and may form dense patches after good rains. It has fleshy spoon-shaped **leaves**, to 10 cm long and 6 cm wide, often tipped with a short stiff point. The highly fragrant, oblong to cylindrical **flower-heads**, to 22 cm long and 5 cm in diameter, appear mostly in late winter and spring. Individual flowers are yellowish-green and covered with woolly hairs mixed with long straight hairs. Qld, NSW, SA, NT.

Silvertails *Ptilotus obovatus*

This spreading shrub-like perennial to 1 m high and across is widespread in inland districts, often on shallow stony ground in mulga communities. The stems and **leaves** are covered with dense star-shaped hairs giving it a whitish appearance. It has obovate to lanceolate leaves, 1–4 cm long and to 2 cm wide, and bears pink **flowers** with long white hairs in ovoid heads to 1.5 cm across. These are borne singly or in groups at the ends of the branchlets sporadically throughout the year, but particularly after rain. Qld, NSW, SA, WA, NT.

Longtails *Ptilotus polystachyus*

This tufted perennial herb to 1 m high is widespread in a variety of sandy habitats and can often be seen growing along the roadside in dry inland areas. The plant is at first covered with short curled hairs, later becoming smooth, and has wavy linear to lanceolate **leaves** to 10 cm or more long. The solitary, sweetly scented cylindrical **flower spikes**, to 15 cm long and to 3 cm diameter, are borne at the ends of long stalks in spring. Flowers are yellowish-green and covered with hairs. There is also a red-flowering form, with purplish-red flowers that turn brown with age. The ovate bracts to 6.5 mm long are straw-coloured with a darker midrib. In the northern part of its range ***P. p.* var. *pullenii*** has broader flowering spikes.

Except for one species which extends to Malaysia, most of the 90 species in this genus are endemic to arid and semi-arid regions of mainland Australia. Qld, NSW, SA, WA, NT.

Most species of *Ptilotus* are easily cultivated in dry, warm sunny gardens with very good drainage.

Amaryllis Family
AMARYLLIDACEAE

Garland Lily *Calostemma purpureum*

This attractive bulbous flowering plant occurs mainly in southern inland districts, where it usually forms scattered colonies along watercourses or on low-lying areas subjected to periodic flooding. It forms a perennial herb to 60 cm high with arching bright green linear **leaves** to about 60 cm long. The leaves die down each year. The reddish-purple or pink **flowers** to 2 cm long are borne in showy terminal umbels of 12–25 flowers on stalks to 50 cm long in summer and autumn. The rounded papery-skinned capsule to 1 cm diameter contains a single fleshy seed which may germinate while still attached to the parent. The Yellow Garland Lily, *C. luteum*, is sometimes treated as a colour variety of *C. purpureum*, but its bright yellow funnel-shaped flowers are longer, up to 3 cm in length, and it may produce up to 30 flowers in each umbel. The genus name is derived from the Greek *calos*, meaning beautiful, and *stemma*, meaning a crown or garland. They are popular in cultivation and are easy to grow in frost-free areas. Flowering is best after dry periods. Qld, NSW, Vic, SA.

The Amaryllis Family, Amaryllidaceae, is closely allied to Liliaceae and genera are sometimes included in the latter family by various botanists. Amaryllidaceae is commonly characterised by the arrangement of flowers in an umbel at the top of a leafless stalk, subtended by 2 fused bracts when in bud. The flowers are often trumpet-shaped and have 6 lobes and 6 stamens.

Daisy Family
ASTERACEAE

Variable Daisy *Brachycome ciliaris*

Found in a wide range of inland plant communities on sand and gibber plains, this spreading herb to no more than 45 cm high will often form dense patches over considerable areas. It has stems covered with short glandular hairs and **leaves** to 5 cm long with 3–9 linear pointed lobes which may be again lobed or toothed. The **flowerheads**, about 3 cm across, have yellow centres with soft white to mauve ray florets and are borne singly on slender stalks in spring to early summer. All States.

Swan River Daisy *Brachycome iberidifolia*

This species is widespread throughout the southern parts of WA and extends into the NT and SA (in spite of its common name). It occurs in a wide variety of habitats and soils, including sand plains and dry water courses. It is an upright annual herb to 50 cm high with light green pinnate **leaves** to 3 cm long with very narrow segments. The **flowerheads** to 2 cm across have central yellow discs and soft white, blue or purple ray florets. They are produced singly on slender stalks in spring and summer. This species is widely cultivated throughout Australia and overseas. SA, WA, NT.

Dwarf Daisy *Brachycome goniocarpa*

This annual herb to 20 cm high is widespread in outback regions where it often appears after good autumn and winter rains. It has weak branching stems covered with fine hairs. The basal **leaves**, to 4 cm in length, may be lobed or divided into narrow segments; the stem leaves are shorter, becoming entire higher up the stem. It has single **flowerheads** to 2 cm across with yellow central discs and soft white ray florets borne on slender leafy stalks to 15 cm long in winter and spring. Qld, NSW, Vic, SA, WA.

Smooth Daisy *Brachycome trachycarpa*

Widespread in inland districts and often on sandy and rocky soils, this is an upright perennial herb to about 40 cm diameter with hairy glandular stems. It has sessile linear **leaves**, 1–3.5 cm long and to 1.5 mm wide, with entire or finely lobed margins. The leaves decrease in size up the stem. Masses of white daisy-like **flowerheads** to 1.5 cm across with yellow centres, are produced singly on slender leafless stalks throughout the year. Qld, NSW, Vic, SA, WA.

Golden Everlasting *Bracteantha bracteata*

(Syn. *Helichrysum bracteatum*) This variable and widespread species is an annual or short-lived perennial herb to about 1 m high. It has dark green, minutely hairy, oblong to narrow–lanceolate **leaves**, to 10 cm long and 2 cm wide, half clasping the stem. The **flowerheads**, about 5 cm across, have a yellow centre surrounded by several rows of shiny petal-like papery bracts that are often turned down at maturity. They appear mostly in spring and summer. The numerous small **seeds** have a crown of fine bristles. This species is widely cultivated as an ornamental garden plant and as a source of long-lasting cut flowers. All States.

Sticky Everlasting *Bracteantha viscosa*

(Syn. *Helichrysum viscosum*) This attractive everlasting occurs naturally on plains and in woodland and can sometimes be seen growing along the roadside on shallow stony soils in semi-arid districts. It is an upright sticky annual or short-lived perennial to 80 cm high with rough, branched stems. The sessile oblong–lanceolate **leaves**, 3–9 cm long and less than 1 cm wide, are dark green and have a varnished appearance. The bright yellow **flowerheads** appear singly or up to 3 together on short stalks in spring. The flowerheads are very similar to *B. bracteata* but are smaller. NSW, Vic.

Calocephalus knappii

This daisy is widespread in dry inland regions where it occurs on red sandy soils. It is a small annual or short-lived perennial herb to 20 cm high with erect or ascending white woolly stems often forming mounds. The stem-clasping linear **leaves**, to 2 cm long and 4 mm wide, are densely covered in white woolly hairs, giving the plant a silvery-grey appearance. Yellow to orange rounded **flowerheads** to 1.5 cm wide are borne at branch ends in winter and spring. Qld, SA, WA, NT.

Yellow Top *Calocephalus platycephalus*

This low-growing white-woolly annual or perennial herb to 45 cm high occurs in sandy soils in arid areas. It has stem-clasping linear to lanceolate **leaves**, to 3 cm long and 2 mm wide, that are smooth to densely hairy. The small yellow terminal **flowerheads**, 1–2.5 cm across, have a slightly flattened top and appear mainly in spring and summer and sporadically throughout the year. The small **seeds** have a distinct tuft of feathery bristles that are joined at the base. Qld, NSW, SA, WA, NT.

Purple Burr-daisy *Calotis cuneifolia*

Widespread on sandy soils in grassland and open forest, this erect or spreading perennial herb to 60 cm high has stems covered with stiff hairs. It has sessile wedge-shaped **leaves**, to 4 cm long and 2 cm wide, with 3–6 pointed lobes near the tip. The **flowerheads** to 2 cm across have yellow centres and white, blue or mauve ray florets. They are produced in great numbers mainly in late winter and spring. The seedheads have 2–4 erect sharp spines attached to each **seed**, forming rounded prickly burrs. Qld, NSW, Vic, SA, NT.

Yellow Burr-daisy *Calotis lappulacea*

Widespread on a variety of soils in woodland, open forest and cleared land, this much-branched subshrub to 50 cm high has wedge-shaped toothed or lobed basal leaves to 6 cm long on young plants, then smaller linear stem **leaves** to 2.5 cm long which may be entire or lobed. The prolific, small yellow daisy-like **flowerheads** to 2 cm across appear throughout the year. Each **seed** has 2 long erect spines and several shorter spreading spines. All mainland States.

Drooping Cassinia *Cassinia arcuata*

This graceful drooping shrub to 2 m high is widespread in a variety of semi-arid habitats in southern Australia. It is invasive and is sometimes given the common name Chinese Scrub because it was often abundant on cleared and disturbed ground adjoining Chinese encampments during early gold-digging days. It has a strong curry-like odour and slender branches covered in fine white hairs. The narrow–linear **leaves** to 1.5 cm long and 1 mm wide have rolled-under margins and a woolly underside. Minute shiny reddish-brown tubular **florets** are produced in terminal drooping panicles to 7 cm long in spring and summer. NSW, Vic, SA, WA.

Cough Bush *Cassinia laevis*

This strong-smelling shrub of light open forest and woodland has woolly white stems 1–3 m high. The narrow–linear **leaves**, 1–5 cm long and to only 1 mm wide, are smooth or slightly wrinkled above with revolute margins concealing a pubescent underside. It bears profuse creamy-white **flowerheads** in loose pyramidal panicles 5–10 cm in diameter at the ends of the branches in spring and summer. It is known to cause irritation to the eyes and throat in some people. Qld, NSW, SA.

Common Everlasting *Chrysocephalum apiculatum*

(Syn. *Helichrysum apiculatum*) This widespread and extremely variable perennial herb grows to 60 cm tall with erect or spreading stems matted with dense woolly white hairs. The linear–lanceolate sessile **leaves**, 1–6 cm long and 1–2.5 cm wide, are also densely clothed in matted hairs. In late winter and spring it bears terminal compact clusters of golden-yellow **flowerheads**, each about 1.5 cm across and surrounded by rows of short pointed petal-like bracts. The small warty **seeds** have a crown of feathery bristles. All States.

Woolly Buttons *Leptorhynchos panaetioides*

This low growing much-branched perennial shrub is usually found growing in heavy clay soils subject to flooding, but also occurs in sandy red soils in mulga country. It grows to 60 cm in height and has sessile, linear to oblong silvery-grey **leaves**, to 1.5 cm long and to 1.5 mm wide, covered with soft woolly white hairs. The yellow dome-shaped **flowerheads**, about 1 cm across, are borne singly on stems 2–5 cm long mostly in spring and summer. The 4-angled **seeds** have a crown of minutely barbed bristles. NSW, Vic.

Minnie Daisy *Minuria leptophylla*

This pretty daisy plant is very common in arid and semi-arid regions where it occurs in many communities, often on sandy and stony soils. It has many spreading or erect stems forming a neat clump to 40 cm high. The bright green narrow–linear **leaves**, up to 4 cm long and about 1 mm wide, are slightly hairy and have a pointed tip. For most of the year, but particularly in spring, masses of white, pink or mauve soft daisy-like **flowerheads**, to 2 cm across, almost cover the foliage. The spindle-shaped **seeds** have a crown of minutely barbed bristles. All mainland States.

Silver-leaved Daisy Bush *Olearia pannosa*

This attractive daisy bush grows mainly in semi-arid open forest and mallee communities in southern Australia. It forms a small shrub to no more than 2 m high with stems and young growth covered with dense white hairs. The broad–oblong or elliptic **leaves**, 3–10 cm long and 1.5–5 cm wide, are entire and deep dull green, sometimes with a thin coating of hair above and silvery hairs below. The white or, rarely, pale mauve **flowerheads** to 5.5 cm across are borne singly on terminal stalks to 30 cm long in late winter and spring. Vic, SA.

Mallee Daisy Bush *Olearia pimeleoides*

Common in semi-arid regions of southern Australia, often in open forest and woodland, this is a compact dome-shaped shrub usually less than 1 m high with greyish branches covered with short woolly hairs. The linear, elliptic or obovate **leaves**, to 2.5 cm long and 1–6 mm wide, are dark green above and grey-woolly below with down-turned margins. Profuse white daisy-like **flowerheads** to 4 cm across are borne singly or in terminal clusters in winter and early spring. The silky-hairy **seeds** are crowned with a tuft of numerous bristles. Qld, NSW, Vic, SA, WA.

Twiggy Daisy Bush *Olearia ramulosa*

This highly variable species is extremely widespread in a variety of habitats in southern Australia It is an aromatic upright shrub ranging from 40 cm to 2.5 m high with greyish-hairy and somewhat sticky young growth and stems. The linear to narrowly obovate **leaves**, to 1 cm long and 2.5 mm wide, are crowded along the stems. They are minutely warty above and woolly below with margins slightly rolled under. Numerous blue, mauve or white daisy-like **flowerheads** to 2 cm across are produced singly along the branches in spring, summer and autumn. Qld, NSW, Vic, Tas, SA.

Azure Daisy Bush *Olearia rudis*

Found in woodland and mallee communities in semi-arid regions of southern Australia, this is a small, somewhat resinous shrub to 1.5 m high. It has bright green elliptic, ovate or obovate stem-clasping **leaves**, to 1.5 cm long and 4 mm wide, that are hairy on both surfaces and may be entire or toothed. The conspicuous pale blue, mauve or purple **flowerheads** to 4 cm across have orange centres and are borne singly or a few together in terminal clusters in winter and spring. The narrow **seeds** are crowned with a tuft of numerous bristles in two rows. NSW, Vic, SA, WA.

Cypress Daisy Bush *Olearia teretifolia*

Mainly from semi-arid regions, this slender sticky shrub to 1.5 m high occurs mostly on sandy soils in mallee, woodland and dry forest. It has many short sticky branchlets. The tiny dark green linear **leaves**, 2–5 mm long and less than 1 mm wide, are slightly grooved beneath and are often pressed against the stem. Masses of small white daisy-like **flowerheads**, 2–5 cm across with yellow centres, are produced in showy terminal clusters in spring and summer. Vic, SA.

Poached-egg Daisy *Polycalymma stuartii*

(Syn. *Myriocephalus stuartii*) Widespread and common in inland sandy habitats, this species is one of the most conspicuous daisies after good autumn rains, often forming extensive yellow and white carpets. It is an erect, often sticky, woolly annual herb 10–50 cm high with linear or linear–lanceolate grey-green **leaves**, 2–7 cm long and 1–5 mm wide, with entire margins and a slightly pointed tip. The large hemispherical **flowerheads** 2–4 cm across have deep yellow disc florets surrounded by several rows of spreading white papery bracts. They are borne atop long stalks in winter and spring. Qld, NSW, Vic, SA, NT.

Drumsticks *Pycnosorus globosus*

(Syn. *Craspedia globosa*) This species naturally occurs in semi-arid regions, mostly in open grassland and woodland. It is grown commercially for its cut flowers which dry extremely well and are widely used in dried arrangements. It is a tufted perennial herb with a basal clump of linear **leaves**, 10–30 cm long and 4–12 mm wide, with a few shorter leaves along the stem. They are covered with dense woolly white hairs on both surfaces giving the plant a silvery appearance. The bright yellow globular **flowerheads** to 2.5 cm in diameter are produced singly on erect stiff stems to 1 m long in spring and summer. Qld, NSW, Vic, SA.

Toothed Ragwort *Pterocaulon serrulatum*

This is an aromatic perennial herb that grows to 90 cm high and has stems and leaves densely covered with a combination of woolly and glandular hairs. The lanceolate to ovate **leaves**, 3–5 cm long and to 2 mm wide, are often toothed and they continue down and form part of the stem. In winter and spring oblong **flowerheads** 2–3.5 cm long, comprising many white to mauve tubular florets, are borne at the ends of the stems. The scented leaves of this very common desert herb are used in Aboriginal medicine to treat colds, flu and sore throats. It is also sometimes chewed as a tobacco substitute. Qld, SA, WA, NT.

Applebush *Pterocaulon sphacelatum*

This rather twiggy, short-lived perennial herb to 1.2 m high is found throughout the outback along dry creekbeds, on low-lying areas, roadsides and wherever else the ground is disturbed. It has stems and **leaves** covered with a combination of woolly and glandular brownish hairs. The oblong leaves, 1–5 cm long and to 1.5 cm wide, are entire or faintly lobed and extend down the stem as wings. They have a strong fruity or apple-like aroma when crushed. Pinkish-white tubular **flowers** form soft spiky balls to 2 cm in diameter at the ends of the stems in winter and spring. Aboriginal people use the leaves to treat colds and wounds. NSW, SA, WA, NT.

29

Sand Sunray   *Rhodanthe tiekensii*

(Syn. *Helipterum tiekensii*) This tufted woolly annual herb to 40 cm high occurs chiefly in mallee country on sandy soils. It has a number of stems arising from the base and grey-green linear **leaves**, 2–6 cm long and 2–6 mm wide. The very small cylindrical yellow **flowerheads** are grouped in globular terminal clusters about 2 cm in diameter in spring. The minutely hairy **seeds** are crowned with a tuft of up to 19 bristles. This species is similar to ***R. moschata***, but the seeds of that species are surrounded by cottony wool and bear a tuft of about 5 bristles. NSW, SA, WA, NT.

Pink Everlasting   *Schoenia cassiniana*

(Syn. *Helichrysum cassinianum*) Widespread in arid and semi-arid outback regions, this small aromatic annual herb to 50 cm high forms extensive colourful carpets, often in mulga and other acacia scrub, following good rains. It forms mostly a basal clump of hairy linear–lanceolate **leaves** that are 3–7 cm long and to 1.5 cm wide, with a few shorter leaves along the stem. Profuse **flowerheads** 2–3 cm across, with yellow centres and surrounded by pink papery bracts, are produced in showy terminal clusters of 5–10 per cluster, usually in spring. Ornamental when in flower, this species is cultivated as a bedding plant and for its pretty cut flowers. SA, WA, NT.

Feathery Groundsel *Senecio anethifolius*

This erect aromatic shrub to 1 m high occurs mainly in arid regions, often on rocky, sandy soils among mulga. The alternate pinnate **leaves**, 5–8 cm long and 2–5 cm wide, are divided into 7–15 narrow–linear segments that are sometimes further divided. Numerous yellow **flowerheads**, each consisting of about 10 tubular petal-less florets about 5 mm long, are produced in compact terminal clusters in late winter and spring. The slender cylindrical **seeds** have tufts of silky white hairs to 1 cm long. NSW, SA.

Annual Yellowtop *Senecio gregorii*

Widespread on red sandy plains in mallee and mulga communities, this colourful annual herb to 40 cm high is particularly abundant in years after favourable autumn and winter rainfall. It has fleshy broad–linear **leaves** 3–9 cm long. The bright yellow **flowerheads**, about 5 cm across, have 8–12 soft spreading petals and are borne singly at the ends of the stems in winter and spring. The dense **seed-head** is composed of numerous slender seeds with long tufts of silky white hairs. All mainland States.

Variable Groundsel *Senecio lautus* subsp. *dissectifolius*

Mainly found in inland districts on a variety of soils, this subspecies will form an erect perennial herb to 70 cm high. It has variable linear **leaves** that are entire or deeply dissected into narrow lobes with entire or toothed margins. The bright yellow **flowerheads**, about 3 cm across, have 8–14 soft spreading petals and are borne in loose clusters at the ends of the branches in winter and spring. All States.

Showy Groundsel *Senecio magnificus*

This erect hairless perennial herb or shrub to 1.5 m high is widespread in inland regions and occurs on sandy alluvial soils near ephemeral streams, along drainage lines and often at roadsides. It has thick or fleshy bluish-green stem-clasping **leaves** 2–7 cm long and 1–3 cm wide, the lower leaves coarsely toothed to entire in the upper leaves. The daisy-like **flowerheads** have 4–8 bright yellow spreading petals with a darker yellow centre and are borne in showy terminal clusters in winter and spring. The **seeds** have tufts of silky white hairs to 1 cm long. All mainland States.

Forget-me-not Family
BORAGINACEAE

Rough Halgania *Halgania cyanea*

Widespread in low-rainfall areas, usually in mallee communities, this is a small sticky shrub to about 40 cm high and spreading to 1 m across. The linear to wedge-shaped **leaves** to 2 cm long and 5 mm wide are toothed towards the tip and covered with flattened glandular hairs. Deep blue or purple **flowers** with 5 spreading lobes to 5 cm across are borne in short terminal clusters throughout the year, more commonly in late winter and spring. NSW, Vic, SA, WA, NT.

Cattle Bush, Camel Bush *Trichodesma zeylanicum*

Occurring in low-rainfall regions on rocky hills, sand dunes, stony alluvial soil or in areas subject to seasonal flooding, this is a coarse upright annual or perennial plant to 1 m tall usually with a covering of long stiff hairs. Stem-clasping linear to narrow–ovate grey-green **leaves**, 4–10 cm long and to 2 cm wide, taper to a pointed tip. Pale blue **flowers**, about 2 cm across, have 5 spreading lobes and are borne in loose clusters at the ends of branches in winter and spring. The plant was eaten by introduced camels in outback Australia. Qld, NSW, SA, WA, NT.

Brunonia Family
BRUNONIACEAE

Blue Pincushion *Brunonia australis*

Endemic to Australia, this monotypic genus is named after Robert Brown, the late eighteenth to early nineteenth century Scottish botanist who studied and described Australian flora. Blue Pincushion is widespread in arid and semi-arid regions and is common over reasonably large areas. When in full bloom it often forms attractive blue carpets along the roadsides where it grows chiefly on sandy and gravelly soils.

The plant is a small tufted annual or perennial herb with leafless silky-hairy stems to about 40 cm high when in flower. At ground level it has silky-soft lanceolate **leaves** 4–10 cm long that are broadest near the tip. Many tiny blue tubular **flowers** with spreading lobes and conspicuous yellow stamens are clustered into heads about 3 cm in diameter. Each head is surrounded by a cup of ovate bracts. Sometimes pale blue flowers are seen. Flowers appear from late winter to early autumn and sporadically at other times. The **fruit** is a small nut. Blue Pincushion is an extremely beautiful ornamental species that is best grown from fresh seed. All States.

Senna Family
CAESALPINIACEAE

Senna artemisioides

(Syn. *Cassia artemisioides*) Widespread in inland districts, this variable species has a confusing range of hybrid forms and subspecies.

Silver Cassia *Senna artemisioides* subsp. *artemisioides*

An erect silvery shrub 1–2 m high with pinnate **leaves** 2–4 cm long that are divided into 2–8 pairs of grey-green or silvery leaflets, each leaflet terete or linear with incurved margins and a flat gland between the lowest pair of leaflets. Bright yellow **flowers** to 1.5 cm across are borne in axillary clusters in winter and spring, followed by flat oblong **pods**, 4–8 cm long and to 1 cm wide. Qld, NSW, SA, WA, NT.

Desert Cassia *Senna artemisioides* subsp. *filifolia*

(Syn. *Cassia eremophila* var. *eremophila*) A shrub 1–3 m high with pinnate **leaves** 4–8 cm long that are divided into 1–4 pairs of terete leaflets that are sparsely hairy when young. Bright yellow buttercup-like **flowers** with 5 petals are borne in short axillary racemes in late winter and spring. Thin flat **pods**, 2–8 cm long and less than 1 cm wide, follow. All mainland States.

Blunt-leaved Cassia *Senna artemisioides* subsp. *helmsii*

(Syn. *Cassia helmsii*) Found in sandy and skeletal type soils, this small bushy shrub to 80 cm high has grey-green pinnate **leaves**, divided into 2–4 pairs of ovate leaflets with a dense woolly covering and a blunt or notched tip. Yellow buttercup-like **flowers** are borne in umbel-like clusters in winter and spring and are followed by broad oblong **pods**, 2–4 cm long and to 2 cm wide. Qld, NSW, SA, WA, NT.

Oval-leaf Cassia *Senna artemisioides* subsp. *oligophylla*

(Syn. *Cassia oligophylla*) This spreading bushy shrub to 2 m high and across is widespread in desert regions and occurs chiefly on red sandy soils in mulga communities. The pinnate **leaves** are minutely hairy or waxy and divided into 2 or 3 pairs of ovate leaflets, 1–2 cm long. Masses of bright yellow buttercup-like **flowers** are borne in clusters of 6–20 in the upper leaf axils in winter and spring. It has a slightly curved **pod** to 7 cm long and 2.5 cm wide. Qld, NSW, SA, WA, NT.

Grey Cassia *Senna artemisioides* subsp. *sturtii*

(Syns *Cassia sturtii*; *C. desolata* var. *desolata*) This grey-green shrub 1–2 m high is widespread throughout the inland. It has pinnate **leaves** 3–6 cm long, divided into 2–8 pairs of linear leaflets covered with dense grey-woolly hairs. Golden-yellow buttercup-like **flowers** appear in the upper leaf axils throughout the year. The flat straight **pod**, to 7 cm long and 1 cm wide, is hairless. Qld, NSW, SA, WA, NT.

Senna artemisioides subsp. *zygophylla*

(Syn. *Cassia eremophila* var. *zygophylla*) This erect shrub 1–3 m high occurs mostly on inland plains and rocky slopes. It has pinnate **leaves** 4–8 cm long with 1–2 pairs of linear leaflets, each about 4 cm long and initially downy but becoming smooth with age. Bright yellow buttercup-like **flowers** about 1.5 cm across appear in short axillary clusters in winter and spring. The thin flat **pod** is less than 1 cm wide. All mainland States.

Cockroach Bush *Senna notabilis*

(Syn. *Cassia notabilis*) Occurring mainly on sandy and gravelly soil and easily seen when fruiting heavily, this is a small spreading shrub to 1.5 m high densely covered with long and short hairs. The pinnate **leaves** are divided into 6–12 pairs of ovate leaflets, each of which is 1.5–4.5 cm long and to 1.5 cm wide, ending with a small bristle. From mid-autumn through to late winter, showy bright yellow **flowers** are produced in erect spike-like racemes held well above the leaves. The distinctive black and yellowish oblong **pod**, to 4 cm long and 1.5 cm wide, has raised ridges over the seeds and resembles a cockroach. Qld, WA, NT.

Fire Bush *Senna pleurocarpa*

(Syn. *Cassia pleurocarpa*) This straggly and often suckering hairless shrub 1–3 m high is widespread in inland sandy areas where it sometimes forms colonies. It has pinnate **leaves** 7–15 cm long, divided into 5–7 pairs of linear or oblong yellowish-green leaflets, each 2–5 cm long and 1 cm wide. The showy yellow **flowers** appear in erect spike-like racemes 7–25 cm long sporadically throughout the year. It has smooth and flat oblong **pods** 3–7 cm long with longitudinal ridges along each side. Qld, NSW, SA, WA, NT.

Bluebell Family
CAMPANULACEAE

Tufted Bluebell *Wahlenbergia communis*

This is a widespread species found in many open situations, often on sandy soils. It is a small tufted perennial herb to 75 cm high with numerous wiry stems and alternate linear **leaves**, to 8 cm long and 6 mm wide, with entire or slightly toothed margins. The blue or sometimes white bell-shaped **flowers** have 5 spreading lobes to about 1.5 cm across and appear over a long period throughout the year, except during the cooler months. The **seed capsule** is elongated and about 1 cm long. All mainland States.

Tall Bluebell *Wahlenbergia stricta*

Widespread from the coast to further inland and common in woodland and open forest, this is a rather robust perennial herb to 90 cm tall with a few branched stems and opposite and oblanceolate lower **leaves** to 7 cm long, becoming alternate and linear up the stem. The bell-shaped **flowers** are blue within and sometimes paler on the outside, 2–3 cm across, and appear mostly in late winter and spring. The **seed capsule** is globular to egg-shaped to 1 cm long. Qld, NSW, Vic, SA, WA.

Caper Family
CAPPARIDACEAE

Wild Orange *Capparis mitchellii*

Widespread in inland Australia, this is a large branching shrub or small tree to 5 m high with a short dark trunk and a broad rounded crown. Young plants are straggly and armed with pairs of small curved spines at the base of the leaves to help with support during the formative years. Older trees are less thorny. The leathery grey-green ovate **leaves**, to 6 cm long and 3 cm wide, are often broadest near the tip and end in a small point. The foliage is palatable and it is valued as a fodder tree. It produces large showy pale yellow **flowers** in the leaf axils, chiefly in late spring and summer and sporadically at other times. They have fringed petals to 3 cm long and about 50 long stamens and wither after opening for one full day.

The rounded fleshy **berry** to about 5 cm diameter is borne on a curved stalk to 6 cm long. Its soft pulp is sweet-smelling when ripe and is said to have been eaten by the Aborigines. Wild Orange is sometimes used in modern bushfood. Qld, NSW, Vic, SA, WA, NT.

Saltbush Family
CHENOPODIACEAE

Old Man Saltbush *Atriplex nummularia*

Widespread and common in dry inland parts, usually on saline soils in low-lying situations, this is a large bushy shrub, 2–3 m high and 4–5 m across. It has circular to ovate bluish-grey **leaves** to 2.5 cm long with a whitish scaly covering and entire or shallowly toothed margins. Male and female **flowers** are borne on separate plants. The yellowish-brown male flowers are in small terminal clusters; the greyish-cream female flowers, without petals but with large leafy bracts, are borne in long terminal panicles and followed by fan-shaped or broad–triangular **fruit**. Flowering is mostly spring to early summer and sporadically after rain. This species is palatable to stock and it is an important fodder plant in times of drought. All mainland States.

Cottony Saltbush *Chenopodium curvispicatum*

(Syn. *Rhagodia gaudichaudiana*) This mealy-white scrambling shrub to 1 m high occurs on calcareous soils in open forest and woodland. It has mostly opposite triangular or spear-shaped **leaves** 1–1.5 cm long covered in a silvery layer of hairs. The small creamy **flowers** have a mealy covering and form spike-like clusters up to 10 cm long in summer. The round shiny red berry-like **fruit** is attached to a felted star-like base. NSW, Vic, SA, WA.

41

Climbing Saltbush *Einadia nutans*

(Syn. *Rhagodia nutans*) Widespread and common in many plant communities, this prostrate or scrambling perennial has numerous long trailing stems and narrow arrow-shaped **leaves** to 3 cm long. The tiny creamy-white **flowers** are produced in short terminal or axillary spikes in summer and autumn, followed by round red or orange berry-like **fruit**. The berries are a source of food for a variety of birds in inland areas. This species is palatable to stock, making it a useful forage plant in times of drought. It is also a popular drought-resistant and ornamental cascading plant for dry-country gardens. All mainland States.

Ruby Saltbush *Enchylaena tomentosa*

This attractive succulent shrub is widespread in drier areas where it occurs on all soil types. It reaches a diameter of 1 m and has rather long straggly stems with a close woolly covering and cylindrical fleshy pale green **leaves** to 1.5 cm long. The inconspicuous **flowers** are followed by flattish green then red berry-like **fruits** which are produced in large quantities and are quite showy. They are quite sweet and were eaten by Aborigines. They are also used to produce a dye. All mainland States.

Black Bluebush *Maireana pyramidata*

(Syn. *Kochia pyramidata*) Widespread in drier areas, this dome-shaped shrub inhabits mainly calcareous soils. It will reach up to 1.5 m in diameter and has succulent blue-green terete **leaves** to 5 mm long with a pointed tip and short downy covering. The small solitary **flowers** are followed by winged **fruit** about 1.2 cm across. They are shaped like a spinning top and are at first creamy-green, then brown or black when dry. The foliage is moderately palatable and it is a useful stock feed in times of drought. NSW, Vic, SA, WA.

Pearl Bluebush *Maireana sedifolia*

(Syn. *Kochia sedifolia*) This species is common in dry southern areas where it occurs on calcareous soils, sometimes in pure stands casting a bluish-grey tinge over the landscape. It is a compact shrub to about 1.5 m in diameter with stems densely covered with close woolly hairs and bluish-grey succulent **leaves** to about 8 mm long and rounded at the tip. Axillary pairs of small **flowers** are followed by straw-coloured or pink-tinged **fruit** with a horizontal wing about 1.2 cm across. The fruit turns brown when dry. This species is attractive to grazing stock, particularly during dry periods. NSW, Vic, SA, WA, NT.

Felty Bluebush *Maireana tomentosa*

(Syn. *Kochia tomentosa*) This species occurs on low-lying saline areas and along creeks, where it forms an erect shrub to 1 m high. The stems are clothed with dense woolly hairs and the succulent semi-terete **leaves** to 1.2 cm long are sparsely hairy. The small solitary **flowers** are followed by creamy-green **fruit** with a flattish translucent horizontal wing, about 1 cm across. The fruit turns brown when dry. NSW, WA, NT.

Thorny Saltbush *Rhagodia spinescens*

This widespread and common inland species occurs on a wide range of soils in association with other low shrubs. It forms a bushy shrub to 1.5 m high and has spiny branches and oblong or almost circular **leaves** 1–2 cm long with a whitish bloom and a conspicuous stalk. The foliage is eaten by stock in times of drought. The inconspicuous **flowers** are borne in short panicles in spring and summer and are followed by red berry-like **fruit** to 6 mm diameter. All mainland States.

Galvanised Burr *Sclerolaena birchii*

(Syn. *Bassia birchii*) Widespread in arid regions and often on sandy soils, this is a spreading greyish-white shrub to 1 m in diameter with stout woolly branches and flat obovate **leaves** to 1.5 cm long covered with short white hairs. The tiny **flowers** are followed by woolly **fruit** covering 4–5 spreading hard spines, with 2 or 3 being larger to 9 mm long. There are about 80 species in this genus endemic to Australia. Qld, NSW, SA, NT.

Sclerolaena cornishiana

(Syn. *Bassia cornishiana*) This much-branched woolly-white small shrub 30–60 cm high is common in dry inland areas in slightly saline habitats. It has tangled and wiry woolly branches and ovate to oblong **leaves** to 1.5 cm long. The very hard, thorny, burr-like **fruiting body** to 6 mm diameter is also covered in dense woolly hairs and has 6 horizontally spreading spines to 8 mm long, 5 of them of equal length. Qld, SA, WA, NT.

Family
CHLOANTHACEAE

Lamb's Tails *Newcastelia hexarrhena*

Found in dry central-western areas, often on sandstone, this is an erect greyish shrub to 90 cm high with a dense covering of hairs on its stems and leaves. It has opposite, very woolly lanceolate **leaves** 3–6 cm long with the edges rolled under. The lilac **flowers** are borne in woolly white oblong spikes to 14 cm long in winter and spring. These have conspicuous bracts that are deciduous as the flowers open. WA.

Newcastelia spodiotricha

This small shrub has a dense covering of whitish-grey hairs on its stems and leaves. This makes it very conspicuous in arid central regions where it grows on red sandy soils. It reaches 1–2 m tall and has pairs of broad–ovate **leaves**, 3–6 cm long and to 3 cm wide, with rolled-under margins. Purple or blue **flowers** with showy stamens are borne in cylindrical spikes 3–8 cm long in winter and spring. The small rounded **fruit** is about 3 mm across. Qld, SA, WA, NT.

DILLENIACEAE

Silky Guinea Flower *Hibbertia sericea*

This very widespread species occurs in a variety of habitats from the coast to farther inland, mostly in open forest and heath on sandy soils. In semi-arid regions it may be seen in mallee country. It is an erect or spreading shrub to 1 m high with silky-hairy stems and linear to narrow–lanceolate **leaves**, to 2 cm long and 2–5 mm wide, with rolled-back margins and both surfaces densely hairy. The yellow 5-petalled **flowers** to 3 cm across are crowded in the upper leaf axils from late winter to early summer. They have numerous stamens arranged on one side of the carpels and conspicuously hairy sepals. Qld, NSW, Vic, SA.

Twiggy Guinea Flower *Hibbertia virgata*

This species also has a wide distribution from coastal heath to farther inland in mallee communities. It is a low, spreading to erect shrub to 1 m high with thin and wiry stems covered with short curly white or brown hairs. The dull green linear **leaves**, to 2.5 cm long and 2 mm wide, are smooth or minutely hairy. The almost stalkless bright yellow **flowers** to 2.5 cm across have notched petals and 10–12 stamens surrounding the carpels. They are well displayed and are borne profusely in the leaf axils in late winter and early spring. Qld, NSW.

Pea Family
FABACEAE

Cactus Pea *Bossiaea walkeri*

This interesting leafless shrub to 2 m high and across is found in drier outback areas, often in mallee communities. It has flat and distinctly winged greyish-green stems and tiny **leaves** reduced to scales less than 2 mm long. The red pea-shaped **flowers** to about 1.5 cm long are borne singly on a very fine drooping stalk sporadically throughout the year, followed by flat hairless **pods**, to 6 cm long and 1 cm wide. NSW, Vic, SA, WA.

Green Birdflower *Crotalaria cunninghamii*

Widespread in inland areas and often found growing on red sand dunes and in mulga communities, this is an erect or sprawling shrub with velvety stems 1–3 m high. The ovate **leaves**, 3–8 cm long and 1–4 cm wide, have short velvety hairs on both surfaces. Large green or yellowish-green pea-shaped **flowers**, to 4.5 cm long and streaked with fine purple or black lines, are produced in erect terminal racemes up to 22 cm long in winter and spring. The inflated **pods** are velvety and up to 5 cm long. Qld, NSW, WA, NT.

Yellow Rattlepod *Crotalaria smithiana*

Found on a variety of sandy soils in the dry centre, this dwarf shrub has erect or prostrate densely hairy stems to 50 cm long. It has downy grey-green obovate **leaves**, 1–4 cm long to 2.5 cm wide, with a rounded or slightly notched tip. The yellow pea-shaped **flowers** to 1 cm long, often with fine reddish stripes in the centre, are borne in terminal racemes to 12 cm long in autumn and winter. The club-shaped **pod** is about 2 cm long. As a group the common name refers to inflated pods that when dry rattle with the seeds inside. Qld, NSW, SA, NT.

Gorse Bitter Pea *Daviesia ulicifolia*

This erect prickly shrub 1–2 m high is widespread and common in southern Australia where it occurs in a variety of habitats. It has spine-tipped branchlets and stiff **leaves** that may be heart-shaped to narrow–lanceolate to 2.5 cm long, with a prominent midrib and ending with a sharply pointed tip. The profuse golden-yellow pea-shaped **flowers** with reddish-brown centres, to 1 cm across, are borne singly in small axillary clusters in winter and spring. The flattened triangular **pods** readily distinguish all species of *Daviesia* from other pea-flowered plants. Qld, NSW, Vic, Tas, SA, WA.

Bat's Wing Coral Tree *Erythrina vespertilio*

Although this species is a tree, it is included here because it is common in dry inland regions where it may grow as a medium shrub to small straggly tree. It is deciduous and has thick corky bark and light but strong timber used by the Aborigines to make shields and food carriers. It has trifoliate **leaves** with each leaflet roughly triangular and resembling a bat's open wings. The pea-shaped scarlet **flowers** are produced in dense racemes to 30 cm long and appear mainly while the tree is leafless in winter and spring. The linear **pod** is 5–10 cm long with a pointed tip. Qld, NSW, WA, NT.

Twining Glycine *Glycine clandestina*

Widespread from the coast to farther inland in a variety of habitats, this weak twining perennial plant is often more noticeable in semi-arid regions, scrambling over other bushes. It has slender, faintly hairy stems and **leaves** composed of 3 greyish-green narrow leaflets. The pale mauve to purple pea-shaped **flowers**, about 8 mm across, are borne in loose axillary racemes throughout the year. They are followed by a linear straight **pod** 2–5 cm long. Qld, NSW, Vic, Tas, SA.

Austral Indigo *Indigofera australis*

This species is widespread throughout eastern Australia, and is included here as it is often noticeable in flower when travelling through dry open forests in outback regions. It forms a slender erect or spreading shrub to 2.5 m high with pinnate **leaves** about 10 cm long divided into numerous oblong leaflets, 1–4 cm long to 1 cm wide. In winter and spring the mauve to purple pea-shaped **flowers** to 12 mm across are borne in showy axillary racemes to 15 cm long and are followed by brown cylindrical **pods**, to 4 cm long and 3 mm wide. All States.

Desert Indigo *Indigofera brevidens*

Found in a variety of sandy soils, this small grey-green shrub to 50 cm high spreads or trails to around 1.5 m diameter. It has grey-green pinnate **leaves** consisting of 11–21 small obovate leaflets densely covered with silky hairs and often slightly folded inwards. The small deep pink or purple pea-shaped **flowers** are produced on erect racemes to 25 cm long in the leaf axils in winter and spring. The cylindrical velvety **pod** is about 3 cm long. NSW, SA, WA, NT.

Silver Indigo *Indigofera leucotricha*

This conspicuous small ashy-white shrub to around 1 m high has a wide inland distribution and is often found growing on rocky hillsides and gorges. The whole of the plant is densely covered with white hairs. It has pinnate **leaves** to 5 cm long with 7–17 small obovate leaflets. The small red to purple pea-shaped **flowers** to 1 cm across are produced in short axillary racemes about 5 cm long from late autumn to early spring. The cylindrical **pod**, about 3 cm long, is densely covered with rusty-coloured hairs. Qld, NSW, SA, WA.

Sturt's Desert Pea *Swainsona formosa*

(Syn. *Clianthus formosus*) Widespread in dry parts of inland Australia, this well-known wildflower is a spreading annual or short-lived perennial herb with stems to about 2 m long, densely covered with long fine hairs. It has large pinnate **leaves** to 15 cm long composed of 9–15 obovate leaflets 1–3 cm long that are silky-hairy on the underside. The striking red pea-shaped **flowers** about 9 cm long are borne in erect racemes of 5–6 flowers in the leaf axils mostly in winter and spring. Each flower has a pointed standard with a glossy black dome at the base. The swollen downy **pod**, 4–9 cm long and less than 1 cm wide, contains many seeds. This is a popular garden plant best suited to a hanging basket or raised garden bed where excellent drainage is assured. Qld, NSW, SA, WA, NT.

Smooth Darling Pea *Swainsona galegifolia*

Widespread in a variety of habitats from coastal regions to farther inland, this is a perennial herb with a woody root system and trailing or upright stems to 1 m high. It has pinnate **leaves** 5–10 cm long divided into about 21–29 pairs of smooth linear or narrow–obovate leaflets. The pea-shaped **flowers** are white, purple or dark red and occasionally yellow, about 1.5 cm long, in racemes up to 20 cm long and bearing up to 20 flowers. They appear mostly in spring and summer and are followed by inflated light green leathery **pods** 2–4 cm long with a beaked end. This species and some other Darling peas are associated with the poisoning of sheep, cattle and horses if heavily grazed over a long period. Qld, NSW, Vic.

Darling Pea *Swainsona greyana*

This bushy perennial herb is found mainly on riverbank situations along the Murray River and the Darling River and its major tributaries. It has a deep persistent rootstock and develops several annual stems forming a clump to 1.5 m high. The stems and leaves are somewhat hairy. The pinnate **leaves** 5–10 cm long are divided into 9–25 obovate leaflets, rounded or notched at the tip. White, pink or purplish-pink pea-shaped **flowers** about 2 cm long are borne in showy erect racemes to 40 cm long composed of 20 or more flowers. These appear mostly in spring and are followed by inflated **pods**, 3–5 cm long and about 1.5 cm wide. Qld, NSW, Vic, SA.

Goodenia Family
GOODENIACEAE

Bushy Dampiera *Dampiera adpressa*

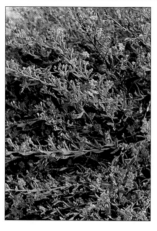

Found mostly in rocky areas in semi-arid regions of eastern Australia, this multi-stemmed perennial shrub to 60 cm high has young stems covered in close white hairs. The entire or faintly toothed ovate **leaves**, 1–5 cm long and to 2 cm wide, are stem clasping. In late winter and throughout spring blue or mauve **flowers** about 2 cm across are borne profusely in groups of 3–5 in the leaf axils. Individual flowers have 5 irregular winged petals united into a short tube in the lower part. This endemic genus is named after William Dampier, who collected plants in Western Australia in the late seventeenth century. Qld, NSW.

Dampiera candicans

This small erect shrub to 70 cm high grows along the roadsides in central Australia, but is fairly ordinary and is only noticeable when you get out of the car to look at other things. Its stems are covered in dense grey to brownish hairs. The elliptic to obovate **leaves**, about 3.5 cm long and 2 cm wide, are shallowly toothed and hairy below. The purplish-blue **flowers** about 1 cm across have petals with narrow wings and a greyish-brown hairy exterior and are borne in loose spikes in autumn, winter and early spring. Its **fruit** is a rounded hairy nut to 2.5 mm long. WA, NT.

Grooved Dampiera *Dampiera lanceolata*

Found mainly in dry forest and woodland in low rainfall regions, this erect perennial sub-shrub to 1 m high has a suckering habit to 2 m across. It has slightly grooved stems and sessile linear to oblong **leaves**, 1–5 cm long and to 2.5 cm wide, with entire or slightly toothed margins and a hairy underside. The deep blue, yellow-throated **flowers** about 1.5 cm across have a dark grey hairy exterior, and are borne in axillary clusters of 3–9 in winter and spring. Qld, NSW, Vic, SA.

Lavender Dampiera *Dampiera lavandulacea*

This short peren-nial subshrub to 70 cm high has prominently ribbed stems covered in short white hairs. It occurs over a wide area in the south-west and farther inland in semi-arid regions where it may form conspicu-ous clumps. It has linear to oblong **leaves**, to 2.5 cm long and about 1 cm wide, with mostly entire rolled-under margins and a hairy under-side. The blue-purple **flowers** to about 1.5 cm across have a yellow throat and hairy exterior and are borne in axillary clusters of up to 3 in winter and spring. WA.

Wild Rosemary *Dampiera rosmarinifolia*

This attractive species occurs in relatively low-rainfall regions in south-eastern Australia, often in sandy soils. It is a downy or densely hairy perennial subshrub with prostrate suckering stems or an upright habit to about 60 cm high. The smooth dark green linear to oblong **leaves**, about 2.5 cm long and 5 mm wide, have strongly rolled-under margins and dense white hairs below. Showy mauve or purple **flowers** to 2 cm across are borne in clusters in the upper leaf axils in winter and spring. Individual flowers have a greyish-white hairy exterior and a yellow throat. Vic, SA.

Cushion Goodenia *Goodenia affinis*

Widespread in dry southern regions, often in mallee country, this low-growing perennial will form a neat mat-like habit to 25 cm or more in diameter. The greyish-felted, mostly basal **leaves** are obovate or spoon-shaped and up to 10 cm long with entire or slightly toothed margins. It has yellow **flowers** with 5 deeply split lobes, about 2 cm across, and a woolly exterior. They are borne singly on stems usually a little longer than the leaves in winter and spring. The **fruit** is an ovoid capsule to 1.5 cm long. WA, SA.

Serrated Goodenia *Goodenia cycloptera*

Widespread in dry inland regions and mostly on sandy soils, this is an annual or perennial herb to 30 cm high with softly hairy, ascending to spreading stems. It has large and coarsely toothed obovate to oblong basal **leaves**, 4–10 cm long to 2 cm wide, and smaller and sometimes entire stem leaves. Profuse yellow **flowers** with a hairy throat and exterior, about 2 cm across, are borne singly on stalks to 5 cm long throughout the year. The rounded seed **capsule** is about 8 mm in diameter. Qld, NSW, SA, WA, NT.

Hairy Goodenia *Goodenia lunata*

Following heavy rainfall in dry inland regions, this attractive mat-forming perennial herb to 20 cm high often forms expansive yellow carpets. It has downy stems that may be erect or may spread and take root to form new plants. The mainly basal, linear to ovate **leaves**, 4–12 cm long to 3 cm wide, are toothed or deeply lobed; outer stem leaves are entire. The yellow **flowers** about 2 cm across have a hairy exterior and are borne on thin hairy stalks from the leaf axils in winter and spring. The **fruit** is an ovoid capsule about 1 cm long. All mainland States.

Cut-leaf Goodenia *Goodenia pinnatifida*

Found mainly in dry inland districts in a variety of soils, this erect to spreading annual or perennial herb to 40 cm high may form conspicuous carpets after good autumn rainfall. It has oblong to oblanceolate, mainly basal **leaves**, 5–8 cm long to 2 cm wide, with toothed or narrowly lobed margins. The showy bright yellow **flowers** 4 cm across are densely bearded and borne in racemes or sometimes umbels on stalks to 12 cm long in autumn, winter and spring. The seed **capsule** is ovoid to globular to 8 mm long. Qld, NSW, Vic, SA, WA.

Scaevola parvibarbata

The flowers in this genus are irregular, with the 5-winged corolla lobes split on one side and spread together like a fan. *S. parvibarbata* is widespread in dry inland districts, mostly on sandy soils. It is an erect, densely hairy perennial herb to about 50 cm high with sessile oblanceolate to circular **leaves**, 1–4 cm long to 2 cm wide, often with toothed margins. The lilac or greenish fan-shaped **flowers**, about 2.5 cm long, have a densely bearded throat and a pollen-receiving cup with short white bristles at the base. They are borne in leafy spikes to 25 cm long from late autumn to mid-spring. Qld, NSW, SA, NT.

Mint Family
LAMIACEAE

Austral Bugle *Ajuga australis*

This perennial herb grows to 60 cm high and is found on a variety of sandy soils in woodland and open forest, usually in sheltered or damp situations. It has erect hairy stems and a rosette of ovate to oblong basal **leaves**, 3–12 cm long and to 3.5 cm wide, with toothed or lobed margins. The stem leaves are sessile and smaller. The violet to blue irregular **flowers** have an elongated 3-lobed lower lip and a short upper lip. They are about 1.2 cm long and are borne in axillary whorls of 6–20 flowers in spring and summer. This attractive species is popular in cultivation. Qld, NSW, Vic, Tas, SA.

Streaked Mint Bush *Prostanthera striatiflora*

Widespread in inland regions, often in shaded gullies in rocky situations, this is an erect aromatic shrub to 2 m high with pale green and rather glandular, lanceolate to narrow–lanceolate **leaves**, 1–3 cm long and to 1 cm wlde. The white **flowers**, about 2 cm long, are distinctly 2-lipped with prominent purple lines and yellow markings in the throat. They are borne in the leaf axils or crowded into terminal leafy racemes in winter and spring. Aborigines dry the leaves and use them to poison waterholes in order to stun and easily catch emus. An infusion of the leaves is also used as a medicinal wash. Qld, NSW, SA, WA, NT.

Mistletoe Family
LORANTHACEAE

Drooping Mistletoe *Amyema pendulum*

Widespread from the coast to inland districts, this pendulous stem-parasitic shrub is usually found growing on many species of *Eucalyptus* and some wattles. It has long drooping branches and lanceolate **leaves**, 10–40 cm long and to 2 cm wide, with a pointed tip. The red **flowers** have 5 free petals and are borne in 3–7 groups of 3 (triad) on a common stalk. The central flower of each triad is sessile, a feature that separates this species from the very similar *A. miquelii*. The flowers appear throughout the year. The small berry-like **fruit** has an inner sticky layer that aids dispersal by certain small birds that feed on it. The berries were an Aboriginal food. Qld, NSW, Vic, SA.

Harlequin Mistletoe *Lysiana exocarpi*

This colourful stem parasite is found on a wide variety of hosts mainly in inland regions. It has smooth drooping stems and leathery linear to narrow–oblong **leaves**, 3–15 cm long and to 2 cm wide, with a rounded tip. The red (rarely yellow) tubular **flowers** are sometimes tipped green and to 5 cm long, usually in a 2-flowered umbel on a short common stalk. Flowers appear mainly in summer and autumn and are followed by red or black **fruit** about 1 cm long. All mainland States.

Hibiscus Family
MALVACEAE

Lantern Bush *Abutilon leucopetalum*

Found in dry inland regions, often on rocky slopes, this small shrub to less than 1 m high can be seen growing in the area of Uluru. Its stems are covered with short and long hairs. The ovate to almost circular hairy **leaves**, 2–8 cm long and 3–6 cm wide, have a heart-shaped base and coarsely toothed margins. The bright yellow hibiscus-like **flowers** to 4 cm long have a tubular to bell-shaped ribbed calyx to 2 cm long. They appear mostly in winter and early spring and are followed by angular **fruit**, about 1.5 cm across, that splits into 7–10 segments. Qld, NSW, SA, WA, NT.

Desert Rose *Gossypium australe*

Widespread in central Australia and attractive when in flower, this is an erect shrub 1–2 m high with stems covered with short dense hairs. It has hairy and greyish ovate **leaves**, 3–6 cm long and to 3 cm wide. The hibiscus-like **flowers**, 4–6 cm across, are mostly mauve with a dark red central blotch and a deeply lobed bell-shaped calyx. Flowering is mainly from late autumn to mid-spring. The hairy **capsule**, about 2 cm long, contains many black seeds covered in spreading bristly hairs. Qld, WA, NT.

Sturt's Desert Rose   *Gossypium sturtianum*

Widespread in dry inland regions, and the floral emblem of the Northern Territory, this is an erect open hairless shrub to 2 m high. The calyx, fruit, leaves and some stems are prominently spotted with dark oil glands. The ovate to circular **leaves**, 2.5–6 cm long and to 3.5 cm wide, are usually entire with a pointed tip. Throughout the year it bears solitary pink or mauve hibiscus-like **flowers**, 6–7 cm across, with a dark red central blotch and a 5-lobed calyx. The black-dotted ovoid **capsule**, about 2.5 cm long, splits into 4–5 segments.

This desert plant is highly ornamental with its large attractive flowers with overlapping petals. It is widely planted in the gardens of Alice Springs and inland towns, where it thrives in the hot, dry climate. After good rains, plants may flower for long periods. All mainland States.

Several species of *Gossypium* are cultivated as a source of cotton, which is obtained from the hairy seeds. In Australia almost all of the cotton grown commercially is derived from **G. hirsutum**. It is native to tropical America and the Pacific Islands and has become naturalised in the Northern Territory and in Queensland.

Hibiscus panduriformis

This species occurs in heavy soils along the banks of streams and margins of clay-pans in northern and central Australia. It is a small open subshrub 1–2 m high that shoots from the woody root-stock in spring following favourable rains. It has velvety stems and leaves. The grey-green, broadly ovate to heart-shaped toothed **leaves**, 3–9 cm long and to 8 cm wide, have a pale underside. In autumn and winter it bears profuse bright yel-

low **flowers** with a maroon central blotch, 6–8 cm across, in the upper leaf axils. These are followed by hairy ovoid **capsules** to 1.5 cm long. Qld, WA, NT.

Lifesaver Burr *Sida platycalyx*

This prostrate or low-growing perennial herb with hairy stems and leaves is found in dry inland regions, often on red soils in mulga country. The ovate to circular toothed **leaves** 1–4 cm in diameter are sometimes heart-shaped at the base. In winter and spring solitary bright yellow 5-petalled **flowers**, about 2 cm

across, are borne on long stalks in the leaf axils. The inflated round **fruit** to 2.5 cm diameter has up to 20 spiny fruitlets enclosed within the enlarged calyx. Qld, NSW, NT, WA.

Wattle Family
MIMOSACEAE

Group 1: Wattles with Cylindrical
Flower Spikes and Phyllodes

Mulga *Acacia aneura*

Widespread and very common in dry inland regions, with dark grey, fissured **bark**, the well-known Mulga is a small shrubby tree with a short trunk and spreading or erect branches 4–10 m high forming an erect umbrella-like crown. The upward-pointed leathery grey-green **phyllodes** are linear and flat to terete, 4–10 cm long and to 3 mm wide with a hardened point at the tip. The golden-yellow rod-like **flowerheads** to 3 cm long are borne singly or, rarely, in pairs on short stalks in the axils of the phyllodes. They occur at irregular periods throughout the year, mainly in autumn and especially after good rains, and are followed by rather sticky flat straight **pods**, 2–4 cm long to 1.5 cm wide, with raised net-like veins.

The flat dark brown seeds, often produced in large quantities, are highly nutritious. Aborigines of central Australia roast and grind them for damper. The seeds have become very popular in modern bush food. They have a rich, nutty flavour and are usually steamed or softened in hot liquid, before being used in ice cream, mousse and crème brulée. Wattle seed flour is used in cakes, biscuits and bread.

Green insect galls about the size of a cherry, found on the foliage and known as mulga apples, are also eaten in desert areas. Mulga is an Aboriginal word for a long narrow shield made from the dark brown yellow-grained wood, which is now used mainly for souvenirs and ornamental wood-work. The medicinal steam from a fire made from the leaves and twigs is used to promote health in new-born babies. Qld, NSW, SA, WA, NT.

Yarran *Acacia burrowii*

This free-flowering erect slender tree 6–13 m high is found in dry inland areas and often in rocky places. It has slightly sickle-shaped and often glaucous **phyllodes**, 4–10 cm long and to 1 cm wide, tapering equally at both ends. The golden-yellow **flowers** are borne in cylindrical spikes 2–3 cm long in axillary pairs in winter and spring. The **fruit** is a straight flat linear pod, 5–8 cm long, and to 4 mm wide. Qld, NSW.

Witchetty Bush *Acacia kempeana*

This silvery grey-green medium-sized shrub grows on rocky and sandy soils, often forming low dense stands around Alice Springs and central desert regions. It has oblong, slightly curved **phyllodes**, 5–10 cm long and to 1.5 cm wide, with numerous fine parallel longitudinal nerves. The golden-yellow **flowers** are borne in rather dense cylindrical spikes to 3 cm long, mostly throughout winter, and are followed by flat oblong **pods**, 3–7 cm long and to 1.5 cm wide. Aborigines obtain witchetty grubs from among the superficial roots. The freshly dug grubs are eaten raw or lightly cooked in hot ashes. Qld, SA, WA, NT.

Gold-dust Wattle *Acacia acinacea*

This branched bushy shrub to 2 m high is wide-spread in dry southern regions and is mainly found in woodland and open scrub. Its stems are yellowish-green and the often wavy **phyllodes** are variable in shape from circular to oval to oblong, 5–25 mm long and 3–10 mm wide, ending in a small straight or recurved point. The profuse golden-yellow **flowers** are borne in globular heads of 1–2 per axil on slender stalks to 1.5 cm long in winter and spring. The **pod**, 3–7 cm long and to 4 mm wide, is twisted or spirally coiled. NSW, Vic, SA.

Silver Mulga *Acacia argyrophylla*

Found mainly in the Flinders Ranges and Mt Lofty regions in wood-land and open shrub, this is a highly attractive, spreading shrub to 3 m high with a similar spread. It has hairy stems and young growth, and obovate to almost rounded **phyllodes**, 2–4 cm long to 1.5 cm wide, that are silvery-grey with a golden sheen when young. Golden-yellow **flowers** are borne in large solitary globular heads on stalks to 2 cm long or on short racemes in winter and spring. The dark brown linear **pod**, 5–10 cm long to 1.5 cm wide, is sometimes constricted between the few seeds. SA.

Rough Wattle *Acacia aspera*

Popular in cultivation, this erect or spreading shrub 1–2 m high comes from dry open forests and mallee country where it grows on stony and gravelly soils. It has hairy resinous stems and linear–oblong **phyllodes**, 1–4 cm long and 2–4 mm wide, covered with short glandular hairs and ending in a soft recurved tip. Dense globular heads of golden-yellow **flowers** are produced on thick stalks to 12 mm long, either singly or in 2s or 3s in the axils in late winter and spring. The curved linear **pod**, 2–7 cm long and to 5 mm wide, is clothed with short stiff hairs. NSW, Vic.

Grey Mulga *Acacia brachybotrya*

Widespread in dry inland areas, mainly in mallee country, this bushy spreading shrub 1–4 m high has stems clothed with close silky hairs. It has obovate grey-green **phyllodes**, 1–4 cm long and to 1.5 cm wide, with a rounded tip. Young phyllodes are silky-hairy. Profuse bright yellow **flowerheads** are borne singly, in clusters or on very short racemes at the ends of the branchlets in late winter and spring. The almost straight linear **pod**, 3–7 cm long and to 7 mm wide, is slightly constricted between the seeds. NSW, Vic, SA.

Wallowa *Acacia calamifolia*

Widespread and conspicuous throughout drier areas of south-eastern Australia and often in open woodland, this erect to spreading rounded shrub 2–4 m high has rather slender branches with weeping tips. It has very narrow linear **phyllodes**, 4–12 cm long and 1–5 mm wide, with a hooked point and one small gland near the base. Masses of perfumed golden-yellow **flowerheads** are borne singly, in pairs or in short racemes in the axils in late winter and spring. The narrow **pod** is 8–20 cm long and to 6 mm wide. The seeds form part of the diet of the rare Mallee Fowl. NSW, Vic, SA.

Acacia dictyophleba

Widespread in central Australia, often in sandy areas in open woodland and hummock grassland, this is an erect, rather open shrub 1–4 m high with long arching branches and ribbed sticky stems. The lanceolate **phyllodes**, 2–6 cm long and 5–10 mm wide, have 2–3 prominent longitudinal veins and net-like lateral veins. They are rounded at the tip with a small point. Large, deep yellow globular **flowerheads** are borne singly or in pairs on sticky stalks in the axils from autumn and throughout the winter months. The oblong flattish **pod**, 5–9 cm long and 1.5 cm broad, is light brown and shiny when young. Qld, SA, WA, NT.

Hakea Wattle *Acacia hakeoides*

Branching from near ground level, this spreading shrub 1–4 m high occurs in open woodland and mallee country chiefly in southern parts of the country and is quite common in the Nullarbor region. It has narrow oblong **phyllodes** that are broader towards the tip, 4–14 cm long and 3–12 mm wide, with a prominent midvein and a conspicuous gland on the upper margin. Profuse, bright yellow globular **flowerheads** are produced on extended axillary racemes 2–8 cm long in winter and spring. The dark brown linear **pod** is 7–12 cm long and 4–7 mm wide. Qld, NSW, Vic, SA, WA.

Brigalow *Acacia harpophylla*

Found on the western slopes of the Great Dividing Range, this erect, densely crowned shrub or tree 5–20 m high sometimes forms large thickets. When dense enough this becomes a low impenetrable forest known as brigalow scrub. It has curved silvery-grey **phyllodes**, 10–20 cm long and 7–20 mm wide, with 3–5 rather prominent longitudinal veins. The yellow globular **flowerheads** are produced in short axillary racemes mostly in winter and spring. The curved brown pod is 3–11 cm long and to 1 cm wide. The violet-scented timber is hard, heavy and close-grained and is used mainly for fence posts. Qld, NSW.

Haviland's Wattle *Acacia havilandiorum*

(Syn. *Acacia havilandii*) Widespread in semi-arid regions, usually in mallee and woodland, this erect and spreading shrub 1–3 m high is occasionally tree-like, with a short trunk to 4 m high. It has cylindrical, slightly curved **phyllodes**, 3–9 cm long and 1 mm wide, with a finely pointed tip and 1 or 2 distinct glands present on the margin near the centre. Profuse, bright yellow globular **flowerheads** are borne usually in axillary pairs in late winter and spring. The slightly curved linear **pod**, 4–9 cm long and 2–3 mm wide, is rather leathery. NSW, Vic, SA.

Acacia ixiophylla

Very noticeable when in flower, this species has a wide distribution in semi-arid regions where it is found mainly in open forests and woodland. It forms an erect shrub 1–5 m high with resinous, often hairy stems. The sticky and slightly hairy, oblong–lanceolate **phyllodes**, 2–4.5 cm long and 3–8 mm wide, have 3 or more prominent longitudinal veins, a rounded tip and a small point. Golden-yellow **flowerheads** are carried mostly on short axillary racemes in winter and spring. The smooth and resinous **pod** is curled and twisted, 3–7 cm long and 2–3 mm wide. Qld, NSW, WA.

Umbrella Bush *Acacia ligulata*

Often found in mulga and saltbush areas, this bushy rounded shrub 2–4 m high is quite common on sandhills and is sometimes referred to as Sandhill Wattle. It has rather thick, deep green linear–oblong **phyllodes**, 4–10 cm long and 2–10 mm wide, with a rounded tip ending with a small hard point. The golden-yellow **flowerheads** are borne singly or on short axillary racemes in late winter and spring. The light brown woody **pod** is 3–8 cm long and 4–10 mm wide. The seeds are roasted and ground by Aborigines for making damper. Medicinally, an infusion of the bark was taken as a cough mixture. NSW, Vic, SA, WA, NT.

Kangaroo Thorn *Acacia paradoxa*

(Syn. *Acacia armata*) Forming a bushy prickly shrub 2–4 m high, often with arching stems, and with rigid spine-like stipules to 12 mm long, this species was once grown as a hedge plant and has become a noxious weed for some districts in Victoria. The oblong to lanceolate **phyllodes**, 1–3 cm long and 3–7 mm wide, have wavy margins. From late winter to mid-spring the whole of the plant is covered with large golden-yellow **flowerheads** borne singly or in pairs in the axils on stalks to 2 cm long. The straight or slightly curved flat **pod**, 2–7 cm long and 3–5 mm wide, is softly hairy. Qld, NSW, Vic, Tas, SA, WA.

Coil-pod Wattle *Acacia pravifolia*

Found in semi-arid regions, mostly in woodland and often on rocky hillsides, this erect rigid shrub 1–2 m high has stems covered with short white hairs. It has small irregular triangular **phyllodes**, 4–12 mm long and 3–8 mm wide, with 2–4 longitudinal veins, a rounded upper margin and sharply pointed tip. The golden-yellow **flower**heads are borne singly in the axils in late winter and spring. The dark brown linear **pods**, to 3.5 cm long and 5 mm wide, are strongly twisted or coiled. Qld, NSW, SA.

Golden Wattle *Acacia pycnantha*

Australia's national floral emblem, this highly attractive free-flowering tall shrub or small open tree 3–8 m high is widespread in the drier parts of the south-eastern States. The shiny dark green lanceolate **phyllodes**, 6–20 cm long and 1–5 cm wide, have a strong central vein and numerous conspicuous lateral veins. In late winter and spring profuse large and perfumed golden-yellow **flowerheads** are produced in axillary racemes up to 15 cm long. The leathery linear **pod** is 5–14 cm long and up to 1 cm wide. The bark is a well-known source of tannic acid and is considered one of the best tanbarks in the world. NSW, Vic, SA.

Needle Wattle *Acacia rigens*

Widespread in arid and semi-arid regions, this rounded bushy shrub 2–4 m high is found mainly in mallee country and woodland. It has grey-green, almost needle-like **phyllodes** 3–13 cm long ending in a short straight or slightly bent point. The profuse golden-yellow **flowerheads** are produced 1–4 per axil from late winter to early summer. The curved or twisted **pod** is 4–10 cm long and 2–8 mm wide. The pleasantly perfumed, hard dark-coloured timber was used by Aborigines for making weapons. Qld, NSW, Vic, SA, WA.

Hard-leaf Wattle *Acacia sclerophylla*

A native of drier parts, chiefly found in mallee country and low scrub, this low-branching spreading shrub 1–2 m high often has a much wider spread, to about 4 m across. It has rather sticky branchlets and narrow–oblong **phyllodes**, 1–4 cm long to 3 mm wide, with several longitudinal veins and a sharply pointed tip. Golden-yellow **flowerheads** are produced 1–2 per axil in winter and spring. The linear **pod**, 3–6 cm long to 3 mm wide, is twisted or curled into a circle. NSW, Vic, SA, WA.

Spiny Wattle *Acacia spinescens*

This erect much-branched shrub to 1.5 m high is found in dry southern regions, often on sandy soils. It has ribbed grey-green branchlets ending in spines. Usually the **phyllodes** are absent; when present they are narrow, to 2.5 cm long and 2 mm wide, with a curved or hooked point. From mid-winter to mid-spring stalkless golden-yellow **flowerheads** are borne singly along the stem. The light brown curved linear **pod**, 2–3 cm long and to 3 mm wide, is constricted between the seeds. Vic, SA.

Acacia spondylophylla

Widespread in dry central regions, often on shallow soils in rocky places, this spreading aromatic shrub to 1.5 m diameter has resinous stems covered in stiff white hairs. The whole plant has a curry-like scent and is sometimes referred to as Curry Wattle. It has sticky linear **phyllodes** 1–2 cm long in whorls of 8–14. Golden-yellow **flowerheads** are borne singly in the axils on stalks to 2.5 cm long in winter and spring. The flat resinous **pod**, 3–4 cm long and to 8 mm wide, is twisted. Qld, WA, NT.

Dead Finish *Acacia tetragonophylla*

This multi-branched shrub 1–4 m high is found in dry inland areas in mulga shrub and woodland. It has narrow linear **phyllodes**, 1–4 cm long and to 1 mm wide, often in whorls or clusters with a sharply pointed tip. In winter and spring golden-yellow **flowerheads**, 2–5 per axil, are borne on stalks to 1.5 cm

long. The strongly curved or twisted linear **pod** is 6–10 cm long and to 8 mm wide. The seeds are roasted and ground by Aborigines for making damper. Medicinally, an infusion of the inner bark was taken as a cough medicine and the fine needle-like phyllodes are used to remove warts. The prickly nature of this plant will bring the unwary traveller to a 'dead finish'. Qld, NSW, SA, WA, NT.

Golden-top Wattle *Acacia tindaleae*

A native of semi-arid regions and often found in mallee country, this erect dense shrub 1–2 m high is common in the Pilliga scrub. It has hairy stems and very hairy, crowded grey-green linear **phyllodes**, 6–12 mm long and 1–2 mm wide, with a rounded tip ending with a small point. It is extremely attractive in flower, when masses of perfumed golden-yellow **flowerheads** are borne singly on hairy stalks to 13 mm long in winter and spring. The brown, straight and flat **pod** is 3–7 cm long and to 1 cm wide. This species is becoming popular in cultivation. Qld, NSW.

Wyalong Wattle *Acacia cardiophylla*

This beautiful species occurs on the western slopes of the Great Dividing Range and is relatively common in the West Wyalong area. It forms a bushy shrub 1–3 m high with hairy stems and bipinnate **leaves** with 8–15 pairs of pinnae and 8–12 pairs of tiny heart-shaped leaflets that are slightly incurved and noticeably hairy. Profuse golden-yellow **flower balls** are borne on single or branched axillary racemes in late winter and early spring. The dark brown **pods**, 3–9 cm long and to 6 mm wide, have long spreading white hairs and are slightly constricted between the seeds. NSW.

Mimosa Bush *Acacia farnesiana*

It is not certain whether this species is indigenous to Australia, or was introduced prior to European settlement. It is a spreading shrub or small tree 3–6 m high with 3–7 pairs of pinnae and 8–20 pairs of small greyish-green linear **leaflets** and 2 very sharp spines at the base of the leaves. Large fragrant golden-yellow globular **flower-heads** are produced 1–3 per axil on stalks to 2 cm long in winter and spring. The round blackish **pod** is 4–6 cm long and about 1 cm wide. It is widely cultivated in Mediterranean countries for the extraction of a violet-scented essential oil used in the perfume industry. Qld, NSW, SA, WA, NT.

Western Silver Wattle *Acacia polybotrya*

Found in inland regions, frequently in seasonally wet situations, this is a tall spreading shrub 2–5 m high. It has bipinnate **leaves** with 2–6 pairs of pinnae and 7–12 pairs of bluish-green oblong leaflets that are usually hairy and about 1 cm long. One small gland is present between the lowest pair of pinnae. Bright yellow ball-shaped **flower-heads** are borne in axillary racemes to 12 cm long in late winter and spring. The slender **pod**, about 7 cm long and to 8 mm wide, is constricted between the seeds. NSW, Qld.

Mudgee Wattle *Acacia spectabilis*

Found mainly on the slopes and plains west of the Great Dividing Range and often in open forest, this is an extremely attractive, erect shrub or small tree 2–6 m high with densely hairy, weeping branches. It has bipinnate **leaves** composed of 2–6 pairs of pinnae and 4–8 pairs of oblong to ovate bluish-green leaflets about 1 cm long. Masses of golden-yellow globular **flowerheads** are carried on long racemes or panicles to 15 cm long in late winter and spring. The ash-coloured **pod** is 5–10 cm long and to 1.5 cm wide. This spectacular flowering species is popular in cultivation. NSW, Qld.

Boobialla Family
MYOPORACEAE

Spotted Poverty Bush *Eremophila abietina*

Endemic to the Laverton district in the Great Victoria Desert, this conifer-like sticky shrub can be seen growing on rocky outcrops. It forms a multi-branched shrub 1–2 m high with rough branches and crowded linear **leaves**, to 2 cm long and 1 mm wide, with a curved pointed tip. The tubular **flowers** to 2.5 cm long are white to pale mauve with purple spots and short hairs. They are produced on long curved stalks in winter and early spring. The calyx remains after the petals have fallen and colours red or bluish-green as it enlarges around the **fruit**. WA.

Narrow-leaved Fuchsia Bush *Eremophila alternifolia*

Widespread in dry inland districts and usually found growing on shallow soils on hills and rocky slopes, this aromatic sticky shrub reaches 2–3 m tall with a similar spread. It has smooth linear to terete **leaves**, 2–5 cm long and to 1 mm wide, with a curved and pointed tip. The deep pinky-red (rarely white or yellow) tubular **flowers** to 3 cm long have a spotted interior and are produced on s-shaped stalks to 3 cm. Individual flowers have 4 upper lobes, 1 lower lobe and broad overlapping calyx lobes. They appear mostly in late winter and spring. The Aborigines use fresh or dried leaves in an infusion for colds, headache and fever. NSW, SA, WA, NT.

Bignonia Emubush *Eremophila bignoniiflora*

This erect shrub or small tree 3–7 m high is found in dry inland districts along watercourses and near waterholes subject to periodic flooding. It has drooping resinous stems and pale green linear–lanceolate **leaves**, 7–20 cm long to 1.5 cm wide. The fragrant 5-lobed tubular **flowers** to 3 cm long are cream with purple or brownish specks and hairy inside. They are produced on sticky stalks to 1.5 cm long in winter and spring. The oval fleshy **fruit**, to 2 cm long, is eaten by emus. Aborigines use the leaves in a body wash to relieve the symptoms of colds and flu. All mainland States.

Silver Turkeybush *Eremophila bowmanii*

Found mainly in inland districts in mulga and mallee scrubland, this erect or spreading shrub to 1.5 m high is densely covered with soft whitish-grey hairs. The densely hairy **leaves** are variable, from linear or ovate to almost circular, 1–5 cm long and to 1.5 cm wide, and have entire curled-under margins. The lilac or blue tubular **flowers** to 2.5 cm long are borne singly on curved hairy stalks in the leaf axils in winter and spring. The densely hairy calyx to 2 cm long is deeply divided into 5 segments. The dryish oval **fruit** is about 7 mm long. Qld, NSW.

Red Rod *Eremophila calorhabdos*

Originally from semi-arid regions in the south-west between Norseman and Salmon Gums, this colourful species has become popular in cultivation. It forms an upright shrub to 2 m high with slender, densely hairy stems and crowded ovate–oblong **leaves**, to 2.5 cm long and 1 cm wide, with toothed margins near the tip. The slender tubular pink or red **flowers** to 3 cm long have pointed and reflexed lobes and are borne on short axillary stalks along the stem, forming a showy leafy spike in spring. The flowers have short calyx lobes. The oval **fruit** is about 7 mm long. WA.

Eremophila christophori

This is a long-flowering species, which occurs naturally in the Macdonnell Ranges in central Australia. It has become very popular in cultivation in dry inland towns. Forming an upright shrub 1–2 m high, it has crowded elliptic **leaves**, 1–3 cm long to 1 cm wide, with a pointed or blunt tip. The blue or mauve tubular **flowers** to 2 cm long have forward-pointed lobes and a hairy exterior. They are borne on very short stalks and crowded in the upper leaf axils, forming a leafy spike from late autumn through to early spring. The narrow oval **fruit** is about 6 mm long. NT.

Slender Fuchsia *Eremophila decipiens*

This species is widespread in southern semi-arid and arid regions and can be seen along the Nullarbor Plain. It is a small, branched, often sticky shrub usually less than 1 m in diameter with linear to lanceolate **leaves**, 2–4 cm long to 1 cm wide, with a pointed tip. The shiny red tubular **flowers**, about 2.5 cm long with a distinct curved-back lower lip, are borne on slender curved stalks along the branches in winter and spring; the smooth calyx lobes are pointed. It has fleshy ovoid **fruit** to 8 mm long. WA, SA.

Eremophila drummondii

This colourful species occurs in semi-arid districts in sand heath or woodland in the south-west. It is an erect shrub 1–2.5 m high with sticky stems and narrow–linear or terete **leaves**, 2–6 cm long and to 1 mm wide, with a pointed tip, that are also sticky. The profuse blue or purple tubular **flowers**, about 2 cm long, are borne 1–2 per axil on slender curved stalks along the branches over a long period in winter and spring. It has fleshy ovoid **fruit** to 7 mm long. WA.

Gibson's Desert Fuchsia *Eremophila gibsonii*

This erect sticky shrub 1–2 m high inhabits sand dunes and ridges in central desert regions. It has smooth shiny stems and sticky light green linear **leaves**, 2–7 cm long and to 2 mm wide, with slightly toothed margins and a hooked pointed tip. The pale lilac, blue or white tubular **flowers**, about 1.5 cm long, have 5 flared lobes, a hairy exterior and are borne 1–2 per axil in winter and spring. The green calyx lobes enlarge after flowering. The ribbed and sticky oval **fruit** is about 6 mm long. SA, WA, NT.

Desert Fuchsia *Eremophila gilesii*

Widespread in central arid regions and usually seen in association with mulga, this small spreading shrub to 1 m high has hairy stems that are sticky when young. It has dark green and smooth, or grey and hairy, narrow–linear **leaves**, 2–6 cm long and less than 5 mm wide, with entire or finely toothed margins and a pointed tip. Blue, mauve, pink or purple tubular **flowers** to 3 cm long with broad pointed lobes have a hairy exterior and a bearded throat; the hairy calyx lobes are pointed. They are borne on S-shaped stalks to 3 cm long in winter and spring. The small rounded **fruit**, about 13 mm long, is hairy. The plant is used in traditional Aboriginal medicine. Qld, NSW, SA, WA, NT.

Tar Bush *Eremophila glabra*

Widespread in semi-arid and arid regions, this is an extremely variable and complex species that may include several varieties or forms. It ranges from a low prostrate form to an upright shrub to 2 m high. The stems are often sticky and may be smooth or covered with dense white hairs. The linear–lanceolate **leaves**, 1–6 cm long and to 2 cm wide, are smooth to densely hairy, mostly with entire margins and a pointed tip. The yellow, orange, pink or red tubular **flowers**, 2–3 cm long, are smooth on the outside or lightly covered with glandular hairs. They have 5 pointed lobes and one distinct curved-back lower lobe, prominently protruding stamens, and are borne on slender curved stalks along the branches sporadically throughout the year. The cup-shaped calyx has 5 short hairy segments. The succulent oval **fruit** is about 1 cm long.

Several ornamental forms of this species are popular in cultivation. A form from the Murchison River area in WA (pictured) is grown for its silvery-grey foliage and scarlet flowers. All mainland States.

Crimson Turkeybush *Eremophila latrobei*

Found in a variety of inland inhabits, this is a variable upright shrub 2–3 m high with warty stems covered in fine hairs. The linear to terete **leaves**, 2–9 cm long and to 5 mm wide, may be smooth or hairy, often warty, with entire and turned-under margins. The red to purplish-red tubular **flowers** 2–3 cm long have pointed lobes and protruding stamens and are lightly covered with glandular hairs; the hairy calyx lobes to 2 cm long enlarge slightly after flowering. The conical **fruit** is about 1 cm long. Aborigines use the leaves in a drink or body wash to relieve the symptoms of colds and flu. Qld, NSW, SA, WA, NT.

Berrigan *Eremophila longifolia*

This tall weeping shrub or small tree, usually to about 4 m high, is found in a wide variety of plant communities throughout the drier parts of Australia. It has warty hairy branches and dull green linear–lanceolate **leaves**, 3–20 cm long and to 12 mm wide, with entire margins and a pointed and hooked tip. The dull red tubular **flowers** to 3 cm long are hairy on the outside and have protruding stamens, a rounded base, triangular calyx lobes, and are produced 1–3 per axil mainly in winter and spring. The glossy rounded **fruit** is about 1 cm long. All mainland States.

Eremophila macdonnellii

Found in central desert regions, this attractive small spreading shrub to about 1 m diameter is named after a nineteenth-century governor of South Australia, Richard G. Macdonnell. It has sparsely to densely hairy branchlets and sessile, green and smooth, or grey and hairy, linear to narrow–ovate **leaves**, to 2.5 cm long and 6 mm wide, with a pointed tip. The deep purple tubular **flowers** to 3.5 cm long are borne on curved stalks to 3 cm long in winter and spring. The succulent rounded **fruit** is about 1.5 cm in diameter. Qld, SA, NT.

Spotted Fuchsia *Eremophila maculata*

This colourful species is a commonly cultivated ornamental. The species originates in inland districts, mostly on heavy clay soils of flood plains of rivers and creeks. It is an erect multi-branched shrub to about 1.5 m diameter with linear to oblanceolate **leaves**, to 4 cm long and 1 cm wide, with entire margins and a pointed tip. The red, orange or yellow slightly curved, tubular **flowers** to 3.5 cm long have a spotted interior, pointed lobes and protruding stamens. They are borne in profusion in winter and spring. The small calyx lobes are triangular and the large rounded **fruit** is to 2 cm long. This species is reported to be poisonous to stock. All mainland States.

Eremophila maculata var. *brevifolia*

This particularly attractive form occurs in arid regions, mainly in mulga scrubland. It reaches about 2 m high and has softly hairy stems and obovate to almost circular **leaves** to about 2.5 cm long with thickened margins. The deep pink or red tubular **flowers**, to about 4 cm long with a rolled-back lower lip, are usually spotted within and are borne on curved reddish stalks to 3 cm long in winter and spring. The rounded **fruit** is around 2 cm across. This variety has been successfully cultivated in dry inland gardens. WA, NT.

Eremophila nivea

This erect silvery-grey shrub to 1.5 m high is found mainly on the sand plains and heaths north and west of Perth. The whole of the plant is covered in dense white hairs. It has linear–lanceolate **leaves** to 1.5 cm long with recurved margins and a pointed tip. The lilac or lavender tubular **flowers**, about 2 cm long, are borne in profusion in the upper leaf axils, forming showy spikes in winter and spring. The small oval **fruit** is about 7 mm long. WA.

Eremophila oldfieldii

Found in south-western arid regions and mainly on red soils, this erect shrub 2–4 m high has sparsely hairy stems and variable lanceolate to narrow–linear **leaves**, to 12 cm long and 1 cm wide, with entire margins and a pointed tip. The red tubular **flowers** to 3.5 cm long have a distinctly curved-back lower lip and are borne on stalks to 1 cm long in winter and spring. The stamens are protruding and the overlapping pointed calyx lobes are green. The oval **fruit** is about 4 mm long. WA.

Eremophila pachyphylla

This attractive species occurs in woodland in semi-arid regions in the south-west. It forms an erect shrub to 3 m high and has narrow–elliptic **leaves**, to 2.5 cm long and 4 mm wide, with entire margins and a hooked pointed tip. The pale mauve-pink tubular **flowers** to 2 cm long are borne on short stalks, 1–3 per axil in winter and spring. The calyx lobes are a darker shade of mauve. The hairy ovoid **fruit** is about 1 cm long. WA.

Flowering Lignum *Eremophila polyclada*

This intricately branched spreading shrub to 2.5 m high occurs in dry inland regions, mainly in low-lying situations subject to flooding. It has smooth and rigid branches and distant linear **leaves**, 2–8 cm long to 3 mm wide, with entire margins and a rounded or pointed tip. Showy white and often lilac-tinged tubular **flowers** to 3.5 cm long are conspicuously spotted and hairy within and are usually borne singly in the leaf axils in spring and sometimes again in autumn. Flowers have smooth green calyx lobes. The almost cylindrical **fruit** is about 1.5 cm long. Qld, NSW, Vic, SA.

Eremophila purpurascens

This species is restricted to the granite hills around Norseman. It forms an erect shrub to 1.5 m tall and has rigid and warty stems. The leathery spoon-shaped **leaves**, to 1.5 cm long and about 5 mm wide, are also warty with entire margins and mostly a rounded tip. It has reddish-purple tubular **flowers** to 2.5 cm long with a spotted interior and protruding stamens, borne on slender curved stalks in winter and spring. The darker coloured and hairy calyx lobes enlarge after flowering. The tiny **fruit** is oblong and about 4 mm long. WA.

Eremophila santalina

Originating in the Flinders Ranges, this beautiful species is popular in cultivation in low-rainfall areas. It forms an erect shrub 2–6 m tall with smooth pendulous stems and dark green lanceolate **leaves**, 3–8 cm long to 8 mm wide, with the tip tapering to a point. Profuse white tubular **flowers** to 2 cm long are borne singly or rarely in pairs on drooping slender stalks about 12 mm long in winter and spring. The calyx lobes have long slender points. The smooth oval **fruit** to 1 cm long is succulent. SA.

Silver Emubush *Eremophila scoparia*

Widespread in southern arid regions, this broom-like shrub to 3 m high is usually found in red sandy soils in woodland communities. The slender branches and leaves are covered with silvery scales. It has linear to terete **leaves**, 1–3 cm long to 2 mm wide, with entire margins and a hooked point. The lilac to white tubular **flowers** to 2.5 cm long are scaly on the outside and have enclosed stamens. They are borne 1–2 per axil on short stalks in winter and spring. The cone-shaped **fruit** is about 5 mm long. NSW, Vic, SA, WA.

Varnish Bush *Eremophila viscida*

This showy free-flowering shrub, 2–5 m high, is widespread in semi-arid regions in the south-west. Its shiny brown stems and leaves are sticky. The light green lanceolate **leaves**, 5–10 cm long and to 1 cm wide, have entire margins that are turned inward and a pointed tip. The profuse pale pink to reddish tubular **flowers**, about 2 cm long, are spotted within, hairy on the outside and have protruding stamens. They are produced in the upper leaf axils in spring. The calyx enlarges after flowering. The oval **fruit** is about 7 mm long. WA.

Western Boobialla *Myoporum montanum*

Widespread in semi-arid regions, mainly in open forest and woodland, this erect bushy shrub to about 4 m high has sticky and sometimes warty stems. The smooth elliptic to lanceolate **leaves**, 3–14 cm long and 2–4 cm wide, have entire margins and a pointed tip. The small white and purple-spotted **flowers** are bell-shaped, with 5 spreading lobes. They are borne 1–7 per axil on stalks to 1.5 cm long in late winter and spring. These are followed by succulent reddish-purple **fruit** to 8 mm across. All mainland States.

Sugarwood *Myoporum platycarpum*

This tall bushy shrub or small tree to 10 m high occurs in semi-arid regions and is fairly common in woodland communities. It has dark grey, deeply fissured bark and sometimes drooping, slender warty branchlets. The glabrous linear–lanceolate **leaves**, 2–9 cm long and 3–12 mm wide, have toothed margins near the tip, which ends in a stiff point. The honey-scented white (rarely pink) bell-shaped **flowers** to 7 mm across are often yellow inside with a hairy throat and have 4 pro-truding stamens. They are produced 2–12 per axil on stalks about 5 mm long in winter and spring and are followed by almost dry ovate **fruit** about 6 mm long.

The whitish sugary substance exuded from wounds made on the branches by insect larvae was once an Aboriginal food and made into sweet drinks. This species is sometimes referred to as False Sandalwood, because when burnt the timber emits a sweet woody aroma resembling that of the commercial Sandalwood, **Santalum spicatum**. Qld, NSW, Vic, SA, WA.

Myrtle Family
MYRTACEAE

Desert Baeckea *Baeckea crassifolia*

Found mainly in low rainfall areas in mallee country, this is a small slender aromatic shrub to 75 cm high with wiry stems and tiny, slightly spreading narrow–obovate to oblong **leaves** 1–3 mm long with a blunt tip. Numerous small tea-tree-like **flowers** to 7 mm across, with 5 rounded pale pink petals and 10 red-tipped stamens, are borne singly on short stalks in the leaf axils in winter and spring. The woody 3-celled **capsule** to 3 mm wide splits open at the top. NSW, Vic, SA, WA.

Scarlet Bottlebrush *Callistemon rugulosus*

This is one of the few bottlebrushes found in outback regions. It occurs mostly on sandy low-lying areas in southern Australia and forms a spreading much-branched shrub to 4 m high and across. It has silky-hairy new growth and narrow–elliptic **leaves**, 3–8 cm long and about 5 mm wide, with prominent oil glands, thickened margins and a sharply pointed tip. The red **flowers** with yellow anthers are produced in spikes, to 10 cm long and 5 cm wide, from late spring through to mid-autumn. The rounded **capsule** is about 1 cm in diameter. Vic, SA.

Fringe Myrtle *Calytrix tetragona*

Widespread throughout southern Australia, this bushy shrub to 2 m high is found from the coast to semi-arid inland regions, where it often forms a heath-like understorey in open forest and woodland communities. It has slender, often arching stems and linear to oblong **leaves**, to 2 cm long and 1 mm wide, often with finely fringed margins. Masses of white to pink star-like **flowers**, about 1.5 cm across, are borne in clusters near the ends of the upper branches in winter and spring. After flowering the calyx lobes become reddish and extend into long hair-like bristles. Qld, NSW, Vic, Tas, SA, WA.

White Mallee *Eucalyptus dumosa*

Widespread in the mallee regions of southern Australia, this tall mallee shrub (rarely a small tree) 2–10 m high has deciduous bark, revealing attractive pale coloured stems. It has grey-green lanceolate **leaves**, 7–10 cm long and 2 cm wide. The yellow-green to reddish cylindrical buds open to white **flowers**, about 1.5 cm across, with up to 7 per axillary umbel. They appear in winter and spring. The cup-shaped **capsule** to 1 cm long has triangular valves that are sometimes at

rim level or slightly protruding. The shallow roots of this species were sometimes drained for emergency water by Aborigines travelling through dry country. NSW, Vic, SA.

Dwyer's Red Gum *Eucalyptus dwyeri*

This mallee shrub or small gnarled tree 5–15 m high is found in semi-arid districts and is locally common in mallee communities. It has smooth cream to grey patchy bark, deciduous in small flakes, and narrow–lanceolate **leaves**, 8–15 cm long and to 2.5 cm wide, dull green on both surfaces. It has often-reddish ovoid buds and creamy-white **flowers** about 2 cm across, 3–7 per axillary umbel in winter and spring. The bell-shaped **capsules** to 7 mm across have protruding valves. This species provides abundant pollen and nectar and yields good honey. NSW, Vic.

Merrit *Eucalyptus flocktoniae*

Found in semi-arid regions in the south-west and also in the Eyre Peninsula, this mallee shrub or slender tree to 12 m high has a smooth light grey deciduous bark, exposing fresh reddish-brown bark. It has dark green and shiny lanceolate **leaves** 8–12 cm long with prominent oil glands. Up to 11 greenish-yellow buds with beaked caps open to abundant nectar-rich creamy-white **flowers** to 2 cm across produced in axillary umbels mostly in spring and summer. The pendulous urn-shaped **capsule** to 1 cm long has slender, slightly protruding valves. SA, WA.

Coarse-leaved Mallee *Eucalyptus grossa*

This beautiful flowering species is fairly common in the Coolgardie and Eyre districts where it grows as a mallee shrub or small straggly tree 3–6 m high. It has rough grey bark on the trunk and smooth reddish upper branches. The thick lanceolate to ovate **leaves**, to 13 cm long and 3–5 cm wide, have a thick yellow midrib and conspicuous lateral veins. The reddish bullet-shaped buds open to large yellow or yellow-green **flowers** to 4 cm across. They are borne profusely in the leaf axils in umbels of up to 7 in late winter and spring. The cylindrical **capsule** to 2 cm long has deeply enclosed valves. WA.

Yellow Gum *Eucalyptus leucoxylon*

Usually a small or medium-size woodland tree with a single trunk, this species can be reduced to a mallee on drier sites. It has deciduous bark shed in irregular flakes. The grey-green lanceolate **leaves**, 7–18 cm long and to 3.5 cm wide, hang vertically in a fairly open crown. Ovoid buds to 1.5 cm long have a short rounded cap. Profuse **flowers**, about 3 cm across, are borne in pendulous clusters of 3 from late autumn to spring. They are usually white or cream, but also pink, red or yellow. The barrel-shaped **capsule** to 1.2 cm long has enclosed valves. NSW, Vic, SA.

Yellow Box *Eucalyptus melliodora*

Regarded by many as one of the best honey producers in Australia, this tree to 30 m high is widespread and fairly common on the western side of the Great Dividing Range. Although mostly a single-trunked tree, it is included here because the sweetly scented honey-laden blossoms are often very prolific and conspicuous and beg to be noticed. It has persistent and fibrous bark on the trunk and lower branches with the upper branches smooth and decid-uous in long ribbons. The grey-green **leaves** are 6–14 cm long. It has club-shaped buds and **flowers** in umbels of up to 7 are produced in spring and summer. Qld, NSW, Vic.

Red-budded Mallee *Eucalyptus pachyphylla*

This highly attractive mallee shrub 2–5 m high grows in red sands in central Australia and can be easily spotted along some of the roads north of Alice Springs. It has multiple stems with greyish bark deciduous in strips revealing smooth pink stems. The ovate to lance-shaped **leaves**, 3-15 cm long and to 5 cm wide, are greyish-green and leathery. It has distinctly ribbed red buds in groups of 3 with pointed caps which fall off exposing showy pale yellow **flowers** to 4 cm across throughout winter to early spring. The hemispherical ribbed **capsule**, about 2.5 cm wide, has a raised disc and protruding valves. Qld, SA, NT.

Red Mallee *Eucalyptus socialis*

This tall mallee shrub or small tree to 6 m high is widespread in dry inland regions, often on sand plains and dunes. It has reddish branchlets and deciduous grey bark revealing smooth white or greyish new bark on the upper stems with persistent fibrous bark at the base. The grey-green lance-shaped **leaves**, 6–10 cm long and to 2 cm wide, have prominent oil dots. It has ovoid buds to 1.5 cm long with an elongated pointed cap. These are shed in winter and spring to reveal masses of creamy-white **flowers** to 2 cm across in clusters of 7–13. The globular capsule to 1 cm long has protruding valves. NSW, Vic, SA, NT.

Coral Gum *Eucalyptus torquata*

Common in the Coolgardie district, this attractive tree to 12 m high can be seen on rocky slopes and hillsides. It has rough dark grey bark on the trunk and lower branches with the upper parts smooth and reddish-brown. The grey-green lanceolate **leaves**, 9–12 cm long and to 2 cm wide, have noticeable oil glands. It has reddish buds to 2.5 cm long with a ribbed base and a long elongated cap. Deep pink or red **flowers** to 3.5 cm across are borne in groups of 7 on slender pendent stalks in spring and summer. The cylindrical **capsule** to 1.5 cm long is distinctly ribbed, with an expanded base. WA.

Homoranthus flavescens

Found mainly in heath and dry forest on the northern table-lands and western slopes and plains, this is an aromatic shrub to about 50 cm high with spreading horizontal branches to 1 m or more across. It has linear to semi-terete **leaves**, to 1 cm long and 1.5 mm wide, with a finely pointed tip. The yellow tubular **flowers** to 7 mm long have a strong, rather unpleasant honey-like scent and are produced in clusters towards the ends of branches in spring and summer. Qld, NSW.

Green Tea-tree *Leptospermum coriaceum*

Found mainly growing on sand dunes in mallee country, this is an erect spreading shrub to 2 m high and across. It has well-spaced ovate to elliptic, thick-textured dull green **leaves**, to 2 cm long and up to 5 mm wide, with a pointed tip. The small white **flowers** to 1.5 cm across have 5 rounded petals and are borne in pairs in the upper leaf axils in winter and early spring. The dome-shaped **capsule**, which has up to 7 or more cells, is deciduous. NSW, Vic, SA.

Leptospermum erubescens

This multi-branched shrub to 2 m high is widespread in semi-arid inland areas of the south-west where it grows mainly in heath and woodland. It has thick-textured obovate **leaves**, to 6 mm long and 4 mm wide, that are smooth and green or grey-green and silky-hairy. The small open-petalled **flowers** are white or pale pink, about 1 cm across, and are produced singly or in pairs at branch ends in winter and spring. The 5-celled dome-shaped hairy **capsule**, about 5 mm in diameter, is deciduous. WA.

Mallee Honey-myrtle *Melaleuca acuminata*

This open wiry shrub 2–4 m high usually occurs as an understorey plant in southern mallee communities. It has pairs of opposite, small, narrow–lanceolate to ovate **leaves**, to 1 cm long and 2–4 mm wide, with a pointed tip. Profuse and sweetly scented creamy **flowers** are produced in lateral clusters of 3–6 flowers on short stalks, usually along the older wood, in spring. The small globular **capsule** is about 4 mm across. NSW, Vic, SA, WA.

Melaleuca conothamnoides

This very attractive shrub can be seen in the Murchison River district of the south-west, growing in sandy heath. It forms a rounded neat bush to 1.5 m high and across and has thick-textured oblong–lanceolate **leaves**, to 4 cm long and about 1 cm wide, with prominent oil glands and a rounded tip ending in a short point. The mauve-purple **flowers** with golden anthers are borne in dense terminal heads to 3 cm diameter in late spring. The **capsules** are fused in a globular cluster around the stem. WA.

Wiry Honey-myrtle *Melaleuca filifolia*

(Syn. *Melaleuca nematophylla*) Occurring naturally in the northern sand plains of the south-west, this highly ornamental species has become a very popular bird-attracting shrub in cultivation. It forms an upright or rounded bush to about 2.5 m diameter and has slightly curved terete **leaves**, 4–10 cm long and 15 mm wide, ending with a pointed tip. Large mauve-purple **flowers** with golden anthers are borne in rounded terminal heads, about 5 cm in diameter, in late winter and spring. After flowering the cup-shaped **capsules** can be seen in rounded clusters. WA.

Scarlet Honey-myrtle *Melaleuca fulgens* subsp. *fulgens*

Well known in cultivation, this beautiful free-flowering subspecies occurs mainly in semi-arid locations in wheatbelt districts of the south-west and is often associated with granite outcrops. It forms an upright shrub 1–3 m high and has linear–lanceolate **leaves**, to 3 cm long and 4 mm wide, with rolled-under margins and a pointed tip. The bright red, orange or pinkish-red **flowers** appear in cylindrical spikes, 3–5 cm long and 4 cm across, on the old wood or from upper leaf axils in later winter and spring. The urn-shaped woody **capsule** is about 1 cm in diameter. WA.

The subspecies **M. f. subsp. *corrugata*** occurs in central Australia and can be seen on rocky hills in the Musgrave Range and westwards to where the borders of SA, WA and the NT meet. It is a small branching shrub to 1 m diameter with crowded opposite linear **leaves**, 7–15 mm long and to 1.5 mm wide, with dark glandular dots on the underside. The white to pale pink **flowers** are borne in spikes to 4 cm long on short lateral branches in spring. It has urn-shaped **capsules** to 1 cm across with a rough wrinkled surface, which is why this subspecies is sometimes called Wrinkled Honey-myrtle. SA, WA, NT.

The bottlebrush-like flowers of the melaleucas often closely resemble those of the genus *Callistemon*. However, the stamens of melaleuca flowers are joined at the base into 5 bundles, while those of callistemons are separate and free.

Inland Paperbark *Melaleuca glomerata*

This bushy shrub or small multi-stemmed tree 2–7 m high is widespread in inland districts and is common along dry creek beds and low-lying areas subject to flooding. It has white papery bark and dark green narrow pointed **leaves**, 2–5 cm long and to 2 mm wide. The pale yellow **flowers** are borne in small globular heads about 1.5 cm across in spring and summer and are followed by clusters of barrel-shaped **capsules** about 6 mm in diameter. NSW, SA, WA, NT.

Melaleuca trichostachya

Widespread in central and inland north-eastern regions, often along watercourses, this is a tall bushy shrub or small multistemmed tree to 4–8 m high with a white and peeling papery bark. It has flat narrow–linear pointed **leaves**, 1–3 cm long and 1–3 mm wide. White **flowers** are produced in loose cylindrical spikes to 4 cm long in spring and summer. The small urn-shaped **capsules** to 4 mm diameter have valves protruding from a wide opening. Qld, NSW, SA, NT.

Broombush *Melaleuca uncinata*

Often forming dense stands, this erect multi-stemmed shrub to 3 m high is widespread in mallee areas of southern Australia. It has needle-like **leaves**, 2–6 cm long and 1 mm wide, with a strongly hooked tip. Sweetly scented pale yellow **flowers** are borne in globular heads, about 1.5 cm across, either in the leaf axils or at branch ends. They appear mostly in late winter and spring and are followed by small, almost globular **capsules** in tight rounded clusters. The upper branches and stems of this species have been used in the construction of brush fences. All mainland States.

Fringed Heath-myrtle *Micromyrtus ciliata*

This very pretty and conspicuous low, spreading or upright aromatic shrub to 1 m high grows in a range of habitats and is common in semi-arid regions in south-eastern Australia. It has minute linear to oblong **leaves**, 1–4 mm long and about 1 mm wide, in opposite pairs at right angles with faintly fringed margins. The tiny cup-shaped **flowers** have 5 petals and 5 stamens. They are white to pink ageing to deep pink and are borne profusely in the upper leaf axils in spring and summer. The **fruit** is a small nut. NSW, Vic, SA.

Coppercups *Pileanthus peduncularis*

This colourful multi-stemmed spreading shrub to 1.5 m high is widespread in the semi-arid northern parts of the south-west region of Western Australia. The opposite, thick, linear to semi-terete **leaves**, 2–4 mm long and about 2 mm wide, have a rounded tip. From late winter and throughout spring bright orange to red **flowers**, about 1.5 cm across, are produced on slender stalks about 2 cm long. They have 5 prominently fringed petals. The **fruit** is a small capsule. WA.

Desert Heath-myrtle *Thryptomene maisonneuvii*

Widespread in arid inland areas, this small spreading shrub to 1.5 m high can be seen growing on sand dunes around Uluru. It has tiny thick obovate **leaves**, to 2 mm long and 1 mm wide, closely packed along the stems. The small white to pink **flowers**, with 5 rounded spreading petals, are produced in the upper leaf axils in winter and spring. The nut-like **fruit** is enclosed in the hardened calyx tube. SA, WA, NT.

Pittosporum Family
PITTOSPORACEAE

Weeping Pittosporum *Pittosporum angustifolium*

(Syn. *Pittosporum phylliraeoides*) This large willow-like shrub or small tree to 10 m high is widespread in inland districts and is found mostly on low-lying areas in mallee woodland. It has narrow–elliptic to oblong **leaves**, 4–12 cm long and 4–12 mm wide, with a distinct hooked tip. The fragrant cream to yellow tubular **flowers** have spreading lobes to about 1.2 cm across and are borne singly or in small clusters from late winter to mid-spring. The ornamental red or orange-red oval **capsule**, about 2 cm long, splits open in two to reveal dark orange-red seeds immersed in a sticky pulp.

This is an important medicinal plant for Aborigines of the inland, who make a rubbing paste from the ground seeds for the relief of sprained limbs, cramps and skin irritations. An infusion of the leaves is taken for the relief of internal pains, and a compress of warmed leaves is applied to induce milk flow in new mothers. The tree also yields a good edible gum.

Being drought-resistant, Weeping Pittosporum is popular in Australia as well as overseas as an ornamental tree for planting in dry areas. The foliage is considered nutritious and is valued as stock fodder during drought periods. The close-grained light-coloured timber is used for making small articles and for wood-turning. All mainland States.

105

PORTULACACEAE

Broad-leaved Parakeelya *Calandrinia balonensis*

Mainly found growing in sandy soils of arid regions, this is a small annual or perennial herb to about 30 cm high with a basal rosette of fleshy linear to lanceolate **leaves**, 5–10 cm long and to 1 cm long. The purple **flowers** have 5 spreading petals and numerous stamens. They are borne on long slender stems and appear mainly in winter and spring. The oval **capsules**, about 1 cm long, contain numerous seeds. The Aborigines used the succulent leaves as a vegetable and as a thirst quencher. Seeds were also ground with water and made into an edible paste. Qld, NSW, SA, WA, NT.

Round-leaved Parakeelya *Calandrinia remota*

This small annual or perennial herb to around 30 cm high grows in sandy red soils of the arid inland. It forms a basal cluster of succulent, almost cylindrical **leaves**, to 11 cm long and 1 cm wide. The deep pink to purple open-petalled **flowers** to about 3 cm across are borne in loose terminal racemes in late winter and spring. The 3-celled oval **capsule** is produced on a drooping stalk to 2 cm long. SA, WA, NT.

Protea Family
PROTEACEAE

Desert Banksia *Banksia ornata*

Banksias are mostly seen in the higher rainfall coastal areas, with one exception, the Desert Banksia, which occurs in south-eastern parts of South Australia and in western Victoria, chiefly in the Big and Little Deserts and usually in deep sandy soils. It forms an erect bushy shrub to 3 m high and has narrow–obovate **leaves**, 3–11 cm long and to 2.5 cm wide, with toothed margins and a lower surface hairy on the midrib. The broad cylindrical **flower spikes**, to 14 cm long and 8 cm diameter, vary in colour from greyish-yellow to velvety bronze. They are produced in the autumn and winter months and are followed by shaggy cylindrical **cones** with persistent spent flowers. Vic, SA.

Spiny Cream Spider Flower *Grevillea anethifolia*

This multi-stemmed shrub to 2 m high is widespread in southern mallee communities, usually in sandy soils. It has velvety branchlets and prickly lobed **leaves** 2–5 cm long divided into 3–5 very narrow linear segments which are again divided. The creamy-white **flowers** are produced in dense umbel-like **racemes** to 2 cm long. They are sweetly scented and profuse during the winter and spring months, often almost smothering the bush. The **fruit** is a small oblong capsule to 8 mm long. NSW, SA, WA.

Rough-leaf Grevillea *Grevillea aspera*

Found in the Flinders Ranges and the Eyre Peninsula in heath and woodland, this is a small dense shrub to 1 m high with velvety branchlets. It has dark green, rough oblong to obovate **leaves**, 3–8 cm long and to 1 cm wide, with a silky-hairy lower surface, recurved margins and a rounded tip ending with a small point. The pinkish-red and cream **flowers** are borne in showy pendent racemes about 4 cm long in late winter and spring. The slightly curved style has a broad green tip. SA.

Flame Grevillea *Grevillea eriostachya*

Found mainly in semi-arid sand plains of western and central Australia, this attractive large open shrub to about 3 m diameter is spectacular when it flowers for many months in winter and spring. It has grey-green, mostly pinnate **leaves** to 30 cm long with narrow–linear segments that become smooth above and grooved and slightly pubescent below. The nectar-rich green to yellow **flowers** are produced in showy one-sided spikes to 20 cm long on long leafless and hairy stems held above the foliage. The prominently winged **fruit**, about 2 cm long, is covered in short dark brown hairs. SA, WA, NT.

Orange Flame Grevillea *Grevillea excelsior*

This species is closely related to *G. eriostachya* and is treated as a subspecies by some authorities. It is found only in Western Australia in southern and central wheatbelt regions. Forming an erect tree to around 6 m high, it has dark green **leaves** to 25 cm long with 3–9 narrow–linear segments. The bright orange **flowers** are borne in terminal one-sided spikes to 20 cm long on long stems, often within the foliage, from early spring to late summer. They are extremely rich in nectar and are a valuable source of food for nectar-feeding birds. The oblong **fruit** is about 2 cm long and 12 mm wide. WA.

Rusty Spider Flower *Grevillea floribunda*

This erect, rather open shrub to 2 m high is widespread in semi-arid areas west of the Great Dividing Range in open forest and woodland, often in stony soils. It has hairy branchlets and oblong to ovate **leaves**, 2–7 cm long and to 2 cm wide, with a matted or silky-hairy lower surface, slightly recurved entire margins and a rounded tip with a short point. The densely hairy greenish-orange **flowers** are borne in terminal pendent racemes to 5 cm long from late autumn to mid-spring; the style is brownish-red with rusty hairs. Qld, NSW.

Honeysuckle Grevillea *Grevillea juncifolia*

Widespread in inland regions on sand dunes and sand plains, this is a spectacular flowering erect shrub 2–6 m high with whitish-grey velvety branchlets. It has slightly pubescent, grey-green linear **leaves** 10–30 cm long that are usually divided into 5 narrow lobes which have rolled-under margins and a sharply pointed tip. The bright yellow to orange **flowers** are borne in erect terminal racemes 7–20 cm long in winter and spring; the style is yellow to orange, to 2.5 cm long. The flowers are extremely rich in nectar which is sucked directly from the flowers by Aborigines or made into a sweet drink. Qld, NSW, SA, WA, NT.

Lavender Grevillea *Grevillea lavendulacea*

From semi-arid southern regions, this is an extremely variable species throughout its range and a number of good flowering forms are in cultivation. It is a low-spreading or upright shrub to 1 m or more high with hairy branchlets and narrow–linear to narrow–obovate **leaves**, to 4 cm long and 1 cm wide, usually with recurved margins and a pointed tip. The pink or red (rarely white) **flowers**, often with paler tips, are massed towards the ends of the branches, forming showy spider-like racemes to 6 cm across in winter and spring. Vic, SA.

Pink Pokers *Grevillea petrophiloides*

This beautiful flowering shrub to 3 m high occurs in northern and inland sand plain regions of the south-west, roughly between the Murchison River area and Merredin. Its stiff **leaves** to 25 cm long are deeply divided several times into linear–terete lobes to about 2 cm long with a pointed tip.

The pink **flowers** are produced in dense cylindrical racemes, about 10 cm long and 3 cm wide, usually at the ends of long leafless stems. They open first from the top and appear mostly from late autumn to mid-spring. The oval, rather sticky and warty **fruit** is about 1 cm long. WA.

Rosemary Grevillea *Grevillea rosmarinifolia*

A popular shrub in cultivation, this extremely variable species comes from scattered locations in semi-arid regions west of the Great Dividing Range. It ranges from 30 cm to 2 m high and has reddish silky-hairy branchlets. The prickly, pointed, linear to narrow–oblong **leaves**, 2–7 cm long to 1 cm wide, have entire and recurved margins and a silky lower surface. A narrow-leaf form was formerly called *G. glabella*.

The pink, red, cream or green **flowers** are produced in terminal pendent racemes to 4 cm across in winter and spring. The well-exserted style is about 2 cm long. NSW, Vic.

111

Sandhill Spider Flower *Grevillea stenobotrya*

Widespread throughout the inland, usually on red sand dunes, this spectacular species is outstanding when in flower in its natural habitat. It forms an open shrub to small tree 3–6 m tall with a rounded or spreading open habit 3–5 m wide. It has leathery narrow–linear **leaves**, 5–25 cm long and to 2 mm wide, with strongly rolled-under margins and a pointed tip. The cream to pale yellow **flowers** are produced in cylindrical racemes 8–25 cm long, with 5–20 racemes grouped together in branched terminal panicles. The flowering period is throughout winter and early spring. Qld, NSW, WA, NT.

Grevillea uncinulata

Widespread in semi-arid inland districts and almost to the southern coast in the south-west, this is a small branched shrub to about 50 cm high with hairy branches and young growth. The narrow–lanceolate to linear–terete **leaves**, to 3 cm long and 3 mm wide, are rough above and hairy below with revolute margins and a hooked tip. Masses of densely hairy cream **flowers** are borne in terminal or axillary umbel-like racemes to 1.5 cm long; the style tip is yellow, ageing to orange or red. Flowers appear in spring. WA.

Bootlace Tree *Hakea chordophylla*

Full of character, this small tree 5–8 m high has an open habit, contorted and pendulous branches and a corky furrowed bark. Widespread in central Australia, it can be seen along the roads north of Alice Springs. The extremely long, dark green, slender and cylindrical **leaves**, 15–40 cm long, droop down from the branches. The showy pendent **flowers**, in large racemes up to 16 cm long, are green at first, opening to greenish-yellow. They are produced on the old wood, mainly throughout winter. The narrow–ovoid **fruit** to 3.5 cm long tapers to a short curved beak. Qld, WA, NT.

Grass-leaf Hakea *Hakea francisiana*

Extremely popular in cultivation, this spectacular flowering shrub or small tree 3–6 m high occurs naturally in semi-arid and arid regions of southern Australia in a wide range of habitats. It has flat silvery-green linear **leaves**, 8–25 cm long and to 6 mm wide, with 5–7 longitudinal veins and a rounded tip with a small point. The deep pink or red **flowers** are borne in erect spike-like racemes to 10 cm long in winter and spring. These are followed by clusters of ovoid **fruit** to 2.5 cm long. SA, WA.

113

Needlewood *Hakea leucoptera*

Widespread in dry inland regions and often found growing on sandy-textured soils in low-lying areas, this is a large bushy shrub or small open tree to about 7 m. It has tough terete silvery-grey **leaves**, to about 8 cm long and 1.5 mm wide, ending with a straight sharp point. Young leaves are often covered with short white hairs, becoming smooth when mature. In spring and summer the creamy-white fragrant **flowers** are borne in showy axillary clusters to 4 cm across consisting of up to 45 flowers. The woody ovoid **fruit**, about 3 cm long and 2 cm wide, is retained on the plant.

    The water-bearing roots of this species were a source of drinking water for central desert Aborigines and explorers. They were dug up, stripped of bark and one end was placed over a slow fire to force the water out the other end held over a container. The roots were also used for making tobacco pipes. The timber is reddish-brown, close-grained and polishes well, and has been used for small turnery articles. All mainland States.

Hakea macrocarpa

This is an interesting small tree to 5 m tall found in central and northern Australia, mostly in open woodland and often on red sand. It has deeply furrowed, dark grey corky **bark** and a rounded crown of thick-textured linear and slightly sickle-shaped, dull green **leaves** to about 20 cm long. Profuse and fragrant greenish-cream **flowers** are borne in dense cylindrical racemes 7–15 cm long in winter and spring. The unusual woody ovoid **fruit**, 3–4 cm long, is swollen in the lower half and splits open on maturity to release the single seed. Although macrocarpa means 'with large fruit', the fruit is not large in comparison to some of the other hakeas.

Aborigines apply the charcoal from burnt pieces of the corky bark to mouth sores and cuts, and the powdered ashes are used to relieve itchy skin. The ornamental flowers are rich in nectar, making this a good bird-attracting plant for dry central-northern gardens that receive seasonal rainfall. It is propagated from seed. Qld, WA, NT.

Hakea scoparia

This beautiful flowering species occurs in inland districts of the south-west, mostly in heath or open woodland. It forms a spreading shrub 1.5–3 m diameter and has stiff, sharply pointed linear to terete grey-green **leaves**, to 20 cm long and 2 mm wide, with 5 longitudinal ridges. The cream, pink or purplish **flowers** are borne in rounded axillary racemes to 4 cm across in late winter and early spring. The beaked ovoid warty **fruit** to 2.5 cm long is produced in clusters. WA.

Long-leaf Corkwood *Hakea suberea*

Common in dry desert regions of the inland, this is a tall shrub or small gnarled tree 3–8 m high with dark brown corky bark. The needle-like grey-green **leaves**, 12–40 cm long, are mostly entire or rarely divided with 2–5 segments. The leaves usually point upwards or out, which separates this species from *H. chordophylla*, which has drooping leaves. Pendulous racemes of creamy-yellow **flowers**, 4–15 cm long, are produced terminally or in the upper leaf axils in winter and spring. The slightly curved woody **fruit** to 3.5 cm long has a prominent beak and sheds its winged seeds annually. SA, WA, NT.

RANUNCULACEAE

Small-leaved Clematis *Clematis microphylla*

This very common and attractive clematis is the most widespread in Australia and is often found climbing on trees and shrubs in mallee country and other dry woodland communities. It is a woody climber with hairy stems to 4 m long. The dull green **leaves** are divided into narrow–oblong leaflets, to 5 cm long and to 5 mm wide. The creamy-white **flowers** have 4 petal-like sepals, are 2–4 cm across and are borne in groups on long slender stalks in the upper leaf axils from mid-winter to late spring. Qld, NSW, Vic, Tas, SA, WA.

Common Buttercup *Ranunculus lappaceus*

Widespread from the coast to the ranges in grassland and forest, this perennial herb to 50 cm high is most abundant in low-lying moist areas. It has softly hairy stems and alternate ovate **leaves** to 8 cm across divided into numerous lobes with toothed segments on slender stalks to 30 cm long. The golden-yellow **flowers** to 3 cm across are borne on erect stalks to 50 cm high. The **fruit** is a globular cluster of 20–50 fruitlets, each with a slender recoiled beak. Qld, NSW, Vic, Tas, SA.

Citrus Family
RUTACEAE

Small-leaf Waxflower *Eriostemon difformis*

Found mainly west of the Great Dividing Range, this aromatic shrub to 2 m high has glandular branchlets. The warty variable **leaves** are linear–oblong, ovate to almost terete, 1 cm long and 2 mm wide. The waxy white or sometimes pink-tinted **flowers** with 5 slightly overlapping petals, to 1 cm across, are produced 1–4 per sessile cluster in autumn and winter. The **fruit** is composed of 4 fruitlets jointed near the base. Qld, NSW, Vic.

Long-leaf Wax Flower *Eriostemon myoporoides*

This pretty flowering species is widespread from the coast to the ranges and to farther inland, chiefly in hilly or mountainous areas. It is a well-rounded shrub to 2 m in diameter with glandular branchlets and dark green narrow–elliptic to oblong **leaves**, 2–12 cm long and to 2 cm wide, ending in a pointed tip. The deep pink buds open to waxy white **flowers** with 5 spreading petals to 2.5 cm across. Profuse clusters of 2–8 are borne from the leaf axils in autumn, winter and spring. Qld, NSW, Vic.

Club-leaved Phebalium *Phebalium obcordatum*

This free-flowering species is found in inland areas of the central east, usually in woodland. It is a small bushy shrub to 1.5 m diameter with warty branches covered with rusty scales. The shiny dark green, oblong to wedge-shaped **leaves** are small, to 4 mm long and 2 mm wide. They are narrowed towards the base, warty or gland-dotted above, scaly below and have a rounded or notched tip. The cream-coloured **flowers** to 1 cm diameter are often profuse and appear in small sessile clusters in late winter and spring. The petals have silvery scales on the outside. The warty **fruit** is about 4 mm long. NSW, Vic.

Narrow-leaved Phebalium *Phebalium stenophyllum*

(Syn. *Phebalium squamulosum* var. *stenophyllum*) Occurring mainly in semi-arid regions in heath and mallee communities in eastern Australia, this erect or spreading shrub to 1.5 m high has scaly brown branchlets. The narrow–oblong to almost terete **leaves**, to 2 cm long and 2 mm or less wide, have rolled-under margins often obscuring the scaly underside. Masses of yellow **flowers** about 1 cm across are borne in sessile terminal heads of 3–10 in spring. The 4 mm **fruit** is composed of 5 fruitlets joined at the base. NSW, Vic, SA.

Hop Bush Family
SAPINDACEAE

Whitewood *Atalaya hemiglauca*

With its outstanding floral and fruiting display, this erect small tree is very noticeable in outback areas. When in flower and fruit, the ends of the branches hang down with the weight. It has a fairly dense crown and rough greyish bark on the trunk. The grey-green pinnate **leaves** are divided into 2–6 narrow–elliptic leaflets, to 15 cm long and 1.5 cm wide. Masses of creamy-white **flowers** with 5 spreading petals are produced in large dense panicles to 20 cm long at the ends of the branches in summer. The 2-lobed **fruit** is a yellowish-green capsule, with distinct wings that grow to 4 cm long. Qld, NSW, SA, WA, NT.

Lobed-leaf Hop Bush *Dodonaea lobulata*

A conspicuous plant in semi-arid parts and often seen in rocky places, this erect, rather sticky shrub 1–3 m high is noted for its colourful reddish capsules. It has shiny narrow **leaves**, 2–5 cm long and to 2.5 mm wide, with numerous small rounded lobes along the margins and a rounded tip. The inconspicuous **flowers**, 2–3 per axillary cluster, appear in late autumn and winter and are followed by highly decorative, deep pink or reddish-brown 2 cm **capsules** with 3 (rarely 4) rounded wings. NSW, SA, WA.

Broad-leaf Hop Bush *Dodonaea viscosa*

Found in all States from the coast to the dry inland, this widespread species is extremely variable in the field and a number of sub-species exist. It is an erect or spreading shrub or small tree 1–6 m high. The mostly sessile, shiny **leaves** may be linear, elliptic to obovate, 1–15 cm long and 1–4 cm wide, with entire or wavy (rarely toothed) margins with a rounded or short blunt point. ***D. v.* subsp. *cuneata*** (pictured) has wedge-shaped leaves. Clusters of small **flowers** are followed by dark pink or purplish-red **capsules** to 3 cm across with 3–4 rounded wings. All States.

Dodonaea viscosa subsp. *angustissima*

This attractive species is widespread in central and southern parts of the continent and is commonly found in open woodland, sand plains and sometimes rocky situations. It is an erect bushy shrub 2–4 m high with sessile, usually sticky **leaves** 3–10 cm long. The **capsule** to 2.5 cm across has 3 (rarely 4) rounded wings. It is produced in great numbers in late winter and early spring and is at first yellowish-green, turning red to purple when mature. The colourful fruit resembles the European hops used in brewing and was used by early settlers as a substitute in beer making. All mainland States.

Small Monkey-flower *Mimulus prostratus*

This annual or perennial prostrate mat-forming plant can be seen in inland districts, usually in low-lying areas that are subject to flooding and margins of swamps that are often saline. It has stems rooting at the nodes forming dense mats to 2 m across. The opposite and sessile obovate to elliptic **leaves**, 2–6 mm long and to 3 mm wide, have entire margins and a pointed tip. The violet or blue **flowers** to 1.5 cm across have a white throat with 5 spreading lobes and are borne singly in the leaf axils mainly in late winter and spring. Qld, NSW, Vic, SA.

Blue Rod *Stemodia florulenta*

(Syn. *Morgania floribunda*) This pretty erect perennial herb to 80 cm high can often be seen in inland regions in low-lying situations, often on saline sands subject to seasonal flooding. It has opposite or whorled narrow fleshy **leaves**, 1–5 cm long and to 5 mm wide, with entire or slightly toothed margins. The bright blue or purple **flowers** with darker streaks have a spreading lower lip with 3 recurved lobes. They are produced singly or in small axillary clusters along the upper part of the stem in spring and summer. All mainland States.

Potato Family
SOLANACEAE

Native Thornapple *Datura leichhardtii*

Widespread in semi-arid inland areas and often found growing along watercourses, this is a fleshy annual herb to around 1 m high with succulent branches and dark green ovate **leaves** to 8 cm long with lobed or toothed margins. It bears creamy-white trumpet-shaped **flowers** to 7 cm long mainly in summer, followed by globular **fruit**, about 2.5 cm in diameter, covered with numerous sharp spines of various lengths and borne on a downward-bending stalk. This species is poisonous to sheep, but animals usually avoid it. Qld, NSW, SA, WA, NT.

Pituri *Duboisia hopwoodii*

Widespread in arid regions of the inland and growing freely on sandy soils and red sandy ridges and dunes, this is a medium to tall shrub to 3 m high. It has slender, often drooping branches and sessile linear **leaves** 5–10 cm long. The small white bell-shaped **flowers**, about 1 cm long with 5 rounded spreading lobes, have purple-striped throats and appear from late winter through to late summer. The **fruit** is a rounded black berry about 5 mm in diameter. The leaves are used by Aborigines to poison waterholes to catch game, especially emus, and as a narcotic. Qld, NSW, SA, WA, NT.

Nicotiana excelsior

Found mainly in central Australia where it grows in rocky gullies and along creek banks, this is an erect leafy herb to 1 m or more high. It has glabrous stems and mostly stem **leaves** that are elliptic to ovate and up to 25 cm long. The leaves at the base of the plant have broadly winged, stem-clasping stalks. The white to yellowish tubular **flowers** have 5 spreading lobes at the tip, but are often closed in sunlight. They appear mostly in winter and spring and are followed by ovoid **capsules** to 2 cm long.

The leaves, flowers and flowering stalks of this species are highly regarded as a chewing tobacco by Aborigines and its distribution is thought to have been spread to WA by them. Several other species of *Nicotiana* were valued as chewing tobacco before the arrival of Europeans. SA, WA, NT.

Kangaroo Apple *Solanum aviculare*

Although mostly coastal, this eastern species is also found farther inland west of the Great Dividing Range. It forms an erect shrub 2–4 m high with ribbed angular stems. Prickles are absent. The **leaves** to 30 cm long vary from deeply lobed with pointed segments to entire and narrow–lanceolate. Entire leaves are usually on the upper parts. The violet-blue **flowers** with spreading pointed lobes to 4 cm diameter are borne in clusters of up to 10 in the leaf axils in spring. The ovoid **berry** to 2.5 cm long is bright orange to red. The ripe berries are eaten by Aborigines. This species is cultivated overseas for the production of steroid drugs. Qld, NSW, Vic. Naturalised in SA and WA.

Shy Nightshade *Solanum cleistogamum*

Widespread in arid regions, often in rocky or gravelly areas or in depressions on sand plains, this annual or perennial herb to 60 cm high has straight slender spines mostly present on its stems, petioles and calyx tubes. The grey-green and densely hairy, ovate to lanceolate **leaves**, 3–10 cm long and 1–4 cm wide, are entire or weakly lobed. Pale lavender **flowers** with rounded petals to 1.5 cm across often remain closed and are produced in summer and autumn. The rounded aromatic **berry** to 1.5 cm across is green or purplish. Qld, NSW, SA, WA, NT.

125

Spiny Potato Bush *Solanum ferocissimum*

This prickly open shrub to 1 m high is scattered throughout arid and semi-arid regions and is often encountered growing in the shelter of other trees and shrubs. It has slightly curved spines on the stems, leaves and flowering stalks. The narrow–linear **leaves**, 3–6 cm long and 2–7 mm wide, are entire or with 1–2 lobes at the base. They are dark green above with a hairy lower surface. White, pale blue or pale mauve **flowers** with 5 spreading pointed lobes to 2 cm across are borne singly or a few together in the leaf axils sporadically throughout the year. The rounded red to black **berry** is to 8 mm across. Qld, NSW, SA, NT.

Round-leaved Solanum *Solanum orbiculatum*

Widespread in central and western desert regions, often on sandy and gravelly soils, this is an erect or rounded shrub to 1.5 m high with densely pubescent stems and leaves. Prickles are absent or sparsely scattered on the stems. The circular to ovate silvery-green **leaves** are to 6 cm long and 3 cm wide. It has purple star-shaped **flowers** to 2.5 cm across, borne singly or a few together in the leaf axils in winter and spring. The globular **berry** to 1.5 cm across is pale yellow, drying to dark brown. The fresh fruit is eaten by Aborigines. SA, WA, NT.

Solanum quadriloculatum

This densely pubescent shrub to 50 cm high is widespread in arid regions, often near seasonally flooded watercourses or on low-lying sand plains. It has a dense covering of greyish stellate hairs and prickles present on stems, leaves, flowering stalks and calyx. Grey-green ovate **leaves**, 5–9 cm long to 4 cm wide, are slightly wavy and densely hairy. The purple **flowers** have spreading pointed lobes to 2.5 cm across and are produced in clusters of up to 20 in winter and spring. When green and immature, the globular **berry** to 1.5 cm across has been suspected of poisoning sheep. Qld, NSW, SA, WA, NT.

Thargomindah Nightshade *Solanum sturtianum*

Widespread and common in inland desert regions, this erect shrub to 3 m high has densely hairy stems. Prickles are scattered or dense on the stems and rarely present elsewhere on the plant. The grey-green narrow–lanceolate **leaves**, 3–6 cm long and to 1.5 cm wide, are slightly wavy. The purple **flowers** have shallowly pointed lobes to 4 cm across and are produced in clusters of up to 12 for most of the year. The globular **berries** to 1.5 cm across are yellowish-brown at first, then black with brittle skin. They are poisonous to both humans and stock. Qld, NSW, SA, WA, NT.

Kurrajong Family
STERCULIACEAE

Crinkle-leaved Firebush *Keraudrenia hermanniifolia*

This prolific flowering shrub is conspicuous in the wheatbelt region of the south-west, growing on sandy or gravelly soils often in northern heaths. It forms a dense multi-branched shrub to 1 m diameter, densely covered with hairs. The oblong to ovate **leaves**, 5–15 mm long and to 7 mm wide, have deep wavy margins, a whitish, densely hairy underside and a rounded tip. The bluish to purple **flowers** have 5 spreading petal-like sepals to 2.5 cm across and are produced in loose clusters in late winter and spring. The flattened **fruit** to about 1.5 cm across is also hairy. WA.

Common Firebush *Keraudrenia integrifolia*

Widespread in inland regions and common in disturbed areas and after fire, this is a bushy shrub to about 1 m high with rusty-hairy new growth. The oblong **leaves**, to 5 cm long and 1.2 cm wide, are finely hairy above and densely hairy underneath. They are slightly concave and have a rounded or notched tip. The petal-less **flowers** have conspicuous bluish to purple sepals to 2.5 cm across in loose terminal or axillary clusters from late autumn through to summer. The rounded **fruit** to 1.2 cm across is densely hairy. Qld, NSW, SA, WA, NT.

Violet Family
VIOLACEAE

Orange Spade Flower *Hybanthus aurantiacus*

This small erect shrub 30–40 cm high is widespread in northern tropical and central arid regions. It has rough and hairy stems and sessile linear to lanceolate **leaves**, to 7 mm long and 5 mm wide, with toothed or sometimes entire margins. The golden-orange irregular **flowers** have 5 petals with 4 very small upper petals, the lowest one largest and spade-shaped to about 1.5 cm long. The flowers are produced singly in the upper leaf axils throughout the year. The fruiting **capsule** is about 9 mm long. Qld, SA, WA, NT.

Shrub Violet *Hybanthus floribundus*

Widespread in semi-arid regions in sandy soils in mallee communities, this is a small shrub to around 1 m high but usually less. It has linear **leaves**, to 3.5 cm long and 7 mm wide, with slightly recurved margins and a pointed tip. The pale blue or mauve **flowers** are produced in clusters in the upper leaf axils from late autumn through to mid-spring. They have a spoon-shaped lower petal to 1 cm long with a prominent spur at the base. The 4 upper petals are small. NSW, Vic, SA, WA.

Grass Family
POACEAE

Barley Mitchell Grass *Astrebla pectinata*

Widespread on inland flood plains, this is a dense tussocky perennial grass to 1 m or more tall with erect much-branched stems developing from short stout rhizomes. It has long and narrow bluish-green flat **leaves** with sharp edges, often becoming curly and twisted with age. The base of the slender spike-like **flowerheads** to 15 cm long may be enclosed in the leaf sheath; the woolly spikelets have conspicuous awns. They are borne well beyond the leaves in spring through to autumn. This very drought-tolerant species is an important forage grass. Qld, NSW, SA, WA, NT.

Comb Windmill Grass *Chloris pectinata*

This smooth-stemmed annual or perennial grass to 30 cm tall occurs in dry inland areas on clayey soils subject to flooding and is common along roadsides. It is shallowly rooted and has mostly basal flat **leaves** 2–3 mm wide. The **flowerhead** is windmill-like with 5–14 slender spreading spikes; the straw-coloured spikelets, about 5 mm long, are crowded along one side of the spike and have a fine hair-like awn 2–3 cm long. They are produced from spring through to autumn. Qld, NSW, SA, WA, NT.

Native Lemon Grass *Cymbopogon ambiguus*

From dry inland regions, this attractive tussock-forming perennial grass to 1 m tall grows along creek banks on coarse sandy soils. The smooth and narrow bluish-green **leaves** to 45 cm long can be red-tinted and often become curly and twisted with age. They have a strong, lemony fragrance. It bears a sparse **flowering panicle** to 35 cm long consisting of a number of pairs of silky-hairy spikes; the blue-green spikelets have awns to 2 cm long. Flowering is mainly in winter and spring. An infusion of dried leaves is used by Aborigines as a rubbing medicine for muscle cramps, skin sores and headaches. Qld, NSW, SA, WA, NT.

Silky Heads *Cymbopogon obtectus*

This tall, strongly aromatic perennial grass is widespread in inland areas. It has smooth stems and narrow bluish-green **leaves** to 30 cm long with sharp edges. The irregularly shaped compact **panicle** to 25 cm long consists of a number pairs of spikes subtended by a smooth narrow leaf-like bract; the reddish spikelets are densely covered with white silky hairs almost concealing the 8 mm long awns. Flowering is mainly in spring and summer. An infusion of the chopped leaves is used by Aborigines for the treatment of colds and coughs. All mainland States.

Silky Bluegrass *Dichanthium sericeum*

This perennial grass to 80 cm tall is widespread across the Australian mainland, in both inland and near-coastal districts. It forms an erect tussock of smooth slender stems with a ring of long white hairs at the nodes. The flat or folded bluish-green **leaves**, 8–15 cm long, are usually hairless, but some forms have a dense covering of white hairs. The **flowerhead**, about 7 cm long, consists of 2–4 erect spikes clustered at the tip of the stem; the numerous pairs of silky-hairy spikelets are crowded along the spikes and have golden-brown awns. Flowering is from early spring to early autumn. All mainland States.

Curly Windmill Grass *Enteropogon ramosus*

This perennial tussock-forming grass to 1 m tall is widespread and common throughout dry regions of mainland Australia. It has flat bluish-green **leaves**, 5–20 cm long and to 6 mm wide, often curled when dry in the tussock. The **flowerhead** consists of 2–14 spikes radiating from the tip of the stem; the spikelets are purplish-brown and compressed along the stem. Flowering is from spring to early autumn. All mainland States.

Woollybutt *Eragrostis eriopoda*

Found over extensive areas in low-lying semi-arid and arid inland regions, this perennial grass to 60 cm tall forms a spreading tussock to 20 cm or more across. The main stems are thickened at the base and covered with dense woolly hairs. It has rigid narrow–linear **leaves** to 8 cm long with a sharp point. The **flowerhead** is a much-branched panicle to 20 cm long; the 2 cm long purplish-green spikelets have 2 over-lapping rows of florets arranged in a chevron-like pattern. Flowers mainly in autumn. Qld, NSW, SA, WA, NT.

Bristly Love Grass *Eragrostis setifolia*

This densely tufted perennial grass to 50 cm tall is widespread in inland regions, where it occurs mainly on clayey soils subject to periodic flooding. It is swollen and hairy at the base. It has numerous slender wiry stems and linear **leaves** to 45 cm long that are inrolled at the base and have sharp and thickened margins that taper to a fine point. The **flowerhead** is an irregularly branched panicle to 10 cm long with numerous green flattened spikelets to 2 cm long. Flowering is mainly in spring and autumn. This species withstands severe drought and is an important pasture grass. All mainland States.

Silky Browntop *Eulalia aurea*

This tussock-forming perennial grass, usually to 50 cm tall, is widespread in inland regions and is often found growing in low-lying depressions and margins of rocky creeks. The finely pointed, narrow flat **leaves** to 30 cm long are bluish-green at first, turning purplish-red in the dry season. The **flowerhead** is an arrangement of 2–4 silky reddish-brown densely hairy spikes, each 5–10 cm long, borne well above the leaves in summer and autumn. When placed over a fire-pit, steam produced from the plant is used as a post-natal therapy in traditional Aboriginal medicine. All mainland States.

Native Millet *Panicum decompositum*

This coarse tussock-forming perennial grass to 1 m tall is extremely widespread and is often found on heavy clay soils in depressions and flood plains. The base of the plant is thickened with several broad loose papery bracts. It has erect hollow stems and flat bluish-green **leaves** to 30 cm long with a prominent white midrib, rough sharp edges and a fine point. The **flowerhead** is a very open panicle to 40 cm long with very small pale green to purplish spikelets. The entire panicle falls at maturity to roll with the wind or flow with water. Flowers appear in summer and autumn. All mainland States.

Feather Speargrass *Stipa elegantissima*

When in flower this grass immediately attracts attention due to its purplish-pink colouring and feathery overall appearance. Feather Speargrass occurs mainly in semi-arid regions of southern Australia.

It forms a perennial tussock to 1 m high

and has stiff slender cane-like stems that are often weeping near the tip. The narrow inrolled **leaves** are somewhat rough to the touch. The soft-looking **flowerhead** is an elongated loose panicle to 20 cm long, consisting of single-flowered spikelets covered with conspicuous pinkish hairs. Flowering is mainly in spring. NSW, Vic, SA, WA.

Kangaroo Grass *Themeda triandra*

(Syn. *Themeda australis*) Widespread across mainland Australia, this tufted perennial grass to 1 m high is found in various grassy woodland communities, often on reddish clay soils and along drainage lines. It grows mainly in spring and summer and has hairless, rather stiff flat **leaves** to 50 cm long at the base and along the stems. The **flowerhead** is a loose panicle to 25 cm long with slender smooth branches and pendulous brownish clusters on long slender stalks consisting of 2–3 spikelets enclosed by a pair of long pointed bracts. Flowering is mostly in spring and summer. All mainland States.

Porcupine Grass *Trioda irritans*

This prickly hummock grass is dominant over vast areas of inland Australia where it is common on sand plains and sandy red soils and on rocky slopes. It forms a compact clump to 60 cm high and 1 m wide, sometimes growing outwards in a distinct ring 1–2 m across. It has sharp spiny grey or bluish-green **leaves** to 20 cm long. The **flowerhead** is a narrow panicle to 20 cm or more long, bearing up to 7 flattened spikelets on thin stalks. Flowering is in spring and early summer. All mainland States.

Purple Plume Grass *Triraphis mollis*

This attractive annual or short-lived perennial grass to 60 cm high is widely distributed in semi-arid and arid regions of inland Australia. It forms small soft clumps and often has a purplish tinge on the stems and flowerheads. The very narrow, smooth and flat or sometimes inrolled **leaves** to 50 cm long taper into a fine point. The soft cylindrical **flowering head** to 25 cm long consists of numerous slender, finely awned and silky spikelets, closely crowded together and often purplish in colour. Flowering is mainly from spring to autumn. All mainland States.

136

GLOSSARY

achene a small, dry, one-seeded fruit that does not split open, as in the daisy family (Asteraceae).
alternate (of leaves) arranged at different levels along a stem; not opposite.

alternate leaves

annual a plant that completes its life cycle from germination to fruiting and then dying within a single year.
anther the top part of the stamen which produces the pollen.
apex the tip of an organ.
arboreal living or situated among trees.
aril the fleshy outer covering of some seeds, often brightly coloured.
awn a slender bristle-like projection.
axil the upper angle between a stem and leaf.
axillary in, or arising from, an axil.
berry a fleshy many-seeded fruit with a soft outer portion.
bipinnate (of leaves) having leaflets growing in pairs on paired stems.

bipinnate leaves

bloom a thin layer of white waxy powder on some stems, leaves and fruit.
bract a small leaf-like structure which surrounds or encloses a flower or group of small individual flowers.
calyx the outer series of floral leaves, each one a sepal.
canopy the topmost layer of branches and foliage of a community of trees.
capsule a dry fruit which when mature dries and splits open to release the seeds.
carpel female reproductive organ, comprising the stigma, style and ovary.
cone a woody fruit of a conifer, made up of overlapping scales; also applied to other woody fruits such as those of banksias and casuarinas.
corolla all the petals of a flower.
crenate (of leaves) the margins scalloped into shallow, rounded teeth or lobes.
crown all the branches of a tree.
deciduous shedding seasonally, e.g. leaves and bark of some trees, parts of the flower.
dentate having coarse, sharp teeth.
disc floret one of the inner tubular flowers of the flowerheads of some Asteraceae, as distinct from the outer ray florets.
drupe a succulent fruit with a stone enclosing one or more seeds.

drupe

elliptic (of leaves) oval and flat, broadest across the middle and tapered equally at both ends.
endemic confined to a specific country, region or location.
entire (of leaves) having smooth margins without teeth or division.
epiphyte a plant that grows on another plant but is not parasitic.
exserted protruding from surrounding parts, e g when the valves project above the rim of a eucalypt capsule.
falcate (of leaves) curved and tapered to a point like a sickle, e.g. many eucalypt leaves.
fissure split.
follicle a dry fruit which splits open along one side only and contains more than one seed.
gall abnormal growth on plant caused by insects.
genus (pl. genera) a subdivision of a family; a group of species that are closely related to each other because they share a number of similarities.

glabrous smooth and hairless.

gland (of plants) a liquid-secreting organ, usually on leaves, stems and flowers.

glaucous covered with bloom, often giving a greyish or powdery appearance.

habitat the place or environment in which particular plants and animals normally live.

incurved (of leaves) curved or bent inwards or upwards.

inflorescence the structure that carries the flowers, which may be arranged in a number of ways, e.g. as a spike or umbel.

involucre leaf-like structure enclosing a flower.

lanceolate (of leaves) shaped like the blade of a lance, usually broadest at the lowest half.

linear (of leaves) long and narrow with more or less parallel sides.

lithophyte a plant growing on rocks.

littoral on or near the shoreline.

mallee 1. shrubby eucalypt with multiple stems arising from an underground rootstock known as a lignotuber; 2. a plant community in semi-arid régions across southern Australia in which mallees are dominant.

margin the edge or boundary line of an organ.

midrib the main central vein that runs the full length of a leaf.

node the point on a stem where one or more leaves arise.

oblanceolate (of leaves) lance-shaped, with the broadest part towards the tip.

obovate (of leaves) egg-shaped, with the broadest part towards the tip.

opposite (of leaves) arising in pairs at the same level, but on either side of the stem.

orbicular (of leaves) circular, or almost so.

ovate egg-shaped.

palmate (of leaves) divided into lobes or leaflets that radiate from the leaf stalk like the fingers on a hand.

panicle an inflorescence with many branches, each of which bears two or more flowers.

peltate (of leaves) circular, with the stalk attached to the middle

panicle

of the lower surface instead at the edge of the leaf.

peduncle common stem that supports a group of flowers or fruits.

pendent hanging down.

perennial a plant with a lifespan of more than two years.

perianth the calyx and corolla of a flower.

petiole the stalk of a leaf.

phyllode a flattened stalk that functions as a leaf, e.g. the leaves of some species of Acacia.

pinna (pl. pinnae) one of the primary divisions of a pinnate leaf (leaflet).

pinnate (of leaves) a compound leaf, divided once with leaflets arranged on both sides of a common stalk.

pod a general term that applies to any dry and many-seeded fruit that splits when ripe to release its seeds, e.g. pods of acacias.

pod

prostrate lying flat on the ground.

pseudobulb the fleshy, bulb-like, thickened stem found on many orchids.

pubescent covered with short soft downy hairs.

raceme an inflorescence where a series of lateral flowers, each with a stalk, is arranged along one stem.

ray floret one of the outer strap-like flowers of an Asteraceae flowerhead.

receptacle the enlarged uppermost part of the flower stalk on which the floral parts are borne.

recurved curved downward or backward.

raceme

reflexed bent downward or backward at a sharp angle.

revolute margins rolled backward to the undersurface.

rhizome a creeping horizontal stem usually gowing either at ground level or just below.

rosette a group of leaves radiating from the same point on a short stem, usually at ground level.

saprophyte a (usually leafless) plant that obtains food from dead or decaying organic matter.

serrate (of leaves) margins having sharp forward-pointing teeth, like a saw.

sclerophyll a plant with hard, stiff leaves.

sclerophyll forest a forested area dominated by trees with sclerophyll leaves, namely the eucalypts.

sepal one of the separate parts of the calyx, usually green and leaf-like.

sessile without a stalk.

shrub a perennial woody plant, usually with two or more stems arising from or near the ground.

solitary (of flowers) occurring singly in each axil.

spathe a large bract enclosing the inflorescence.

spike an unbranched elongated inflorescence with stalkless flowers.

spike

spikelet a grassflower head generally composed of two bracts and one or more florets.

stamen the male portion of a flower, comprised of a pollen-bearing anther and the supporting stalk (filament).

standard the large upper petal of a flower of the family Fabaceae.

stigma the part of the carpel that receives the pollen, usually at the tip of the style.

stipule a leaf-like appendage at the base of the leaf stalk in some plants; usually paired; sometimes modified as spines.

style the stalk of the female organ connecting the stigma and ovary.

succulent fleshy or juicy.

sucker a new shoot growing from the roots of the parent plant.

terete slender and cylindrical in cross section.

terminal situated at the tip.

terrestrial growing on the ground.

tomentose covered with short, closely matted hairs.

toothed (of leaves) a generalised term referring to margins that are **toothed** in various ways, including crenate, dentate and serrate.

trifoliate having three leaves or leaflets.

umbel a cluster of individual flowers where several flower stalks arise from the same point at the top of the main stem.

umbel

valve the segment into which some dry fruits separate when splitting open.

venation (of leaves) the arrangement or pattern of veins.

whorl ring of leaves or floral parts encircling a stem at the same level.

wing (of flowers) the two lateral petals of a Fabaceae flower.

woolly with long, soft, rather matted hairs.

FURTHER READING

Aboriginal Communities of the Northern Territory (1993) *Traditional Aboriginal Medicines in the Northern Territory of Australia*, Conservation Commission of the Northern Territory of Australia, Darwin.

Australian Daisy Study Group (1987) *Australian Daisies for Gardens and Floral Art*, Lothian Publishing Co., Melbourne.

Australian Plants Quarterly, Society for Growing Australian Plants, Sydney.

Australian Systemic Botany Society (1981) *Flora of Central Australia* (ed. J. Jessop), A. H. & A. W. Reed, Sydney.

Beard, J. S. (1990) *Plant Life of Western Australia*, Kangaroo Press, Sydney.

Black, J. M. (1943–57) Flora of South Australia, Parts 1–4, Government Printer, Adelaide.

Black, J. M. (1978) *Flora of South Australia*, Part 1 (3rd edn), Government Printer, Adelaide.

Blackall, W. E. (1954) *How to Know Western Australian Wildflowers*, Part 1, University of Western Australia Press, Perth.

Blackall, W. E. and Grieve, B. J. (1956 –80) *How to Know Western Australian Wildflowers*, Parts 2–4, University of Western Australia Press, Perth.

Chippendale, G. M. (1973) *Eucalypts of the Western Australian Goldfields*, Australian Government Publishing Service, Canberra.

Cribb, A. B. (1981) *Wild Medicine in Australia*, Fontana, Sydney.

Cribb, A. B. and J. W. (1982) *Wild Food in Australia* (revised edition), Fontana, Sydney.

Cunningham, G. M., Mulham, W. E., Milthorpe, P. L. and Leigh, J. H. (1981) *Plants of Western New South Wales*, Soil Conservation Service of New South Wales.

Elliot, W. R. and Jones, D. L. (1980–1997) *Encyclopaedia of Australian Plants Suitable for Cultivation*, Vols 1–7, Lothian Publishing Co., Melbourne.

Erickson, R., George, A. S., Marchant, N. G. and Morcombe, M. K. (1973) *Flowers and Plants of Western Australia*, A. H. & A. W. Reed, Sydney.

Flora of Australia Series (1981–) Australian Government Publishing Service (1981–1994), Australian Biological Resources Study with CSIRO (1995–), Melbourne.

Harden, G.J. (ed.) (1990–1993) *Flora of New South Wales*, Vols 1–4, New South Wales University Press, Sydney.

Hill, K. D. and Johnson, L. A. S. 'Systemic studies in the eucalypts: A revision of the bloodwoods, genus *Corymbia* (Myrtaceae)' in *Telopea* 6 (2–3), 185–469.

Holliday, I. (1989) *A Field Guide to Melaleucas*, Hamlyn Australia, Melbourne.

Isaacs, J. (1987) *Bush Food, Aboriginal Food and Herbal Medicine*, Weldons, Sydney.

Lassak, E. V. and McCarthy, T. (2001) *Australian Medicinal Plants*, Reed New Holland, Sydney.

Olde, O. & Marriott, N. (1994–1995) *The Grevillea Book*, Vols 1–3, Kangaroo Press, Sydney.

Simmons, M. H. (1981) *Acacias of Australia*, Thomas Nelson Australia, Vic.

Specht, R. L. (1972) *Vegetation of South Australia*, 2nd edn, Government Printer, Adelaide.

Whibley, D. J. E. (1980) *Acacias of South Australia*, Government Printer, Adelaide.

INDEX

141